SCHOOL PRAYER

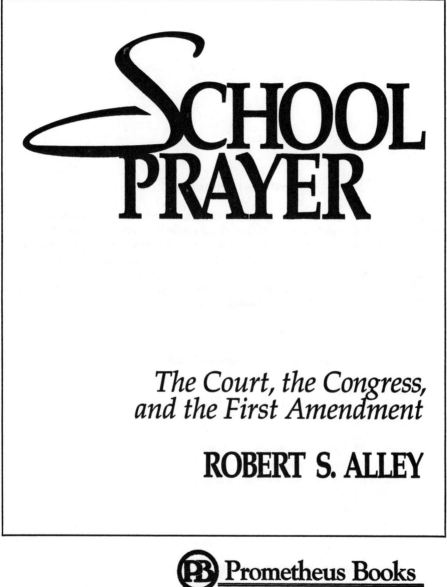

SCHOOL PRAYER

The Court, the Congress, and the First Amendment

ROBERT S. ALLEY

Prometheus Books

59 John Glenn Drive
Amherst, New York 14228-2197

Published 1994 by Prometheus Books

99 98 97 96   5 4 3 2

Library of Congress Cataloging-in-Publication Data

Alley, Robert S. 1932–
    School prayer : the Court, the Congress, and the First Amendment / Robert S. Alley.
        p. cm.
    Includes bibliographical references and index.
    ISBN 0–87975–843–0 (Cloth)
    1. Prayer in the public schools—Law and legislation—United States. I. Title.
KF4162.A94   1994
344.73'0796—dc20
[347.304796]   93–38940
                                                                                 CIP

Printed in the United States of America on acid-free paper

To my brother

Reuben

whose generous spirit, interest, and support
have consistently smoothed my path

Contents

Preface

My earliest thoughts about writing this book came in 1966 with my appearance before the Senate Judiciary Subcommittee on Constitutional Amendments. It seemed to me at the time that the testimony of witnesses on the subject of public school prayer would make a fascinating study. A quarter century later, with an additional dozen volumes of hearings before Senate and House committees, the moment was clearly at hand.

There are numerous persons to whom I owe a debt for assistance, including Rosemary Brevard of the Baptist Joint Committee on Public Affairs, who generously provided me with hard copies of almost all the hearings. Conversations with Steven Green, Rob Boston, and Joe Conn of Americans United kept me abreast of developments on the Hill over the past few months. My father, Reuben E. Alley, editor of *The Religious Herald* from 1937 to 1970, had as much respect for Madison's *Memorial and Remonstrance* as he did for the Bible and never ceased to challenge his own religious assumptions with new scientific and historical knowledge. He questioned everything with a tenacious integrity. My mother, Mary Sutherland Alley, was remarkable as a Christian believer with an unquestioning acceptance of the Bible stories. She never flagged in her encouragement of ideas and opinions in her son, ideas she never personally shared. I can still hear her saying, "I just have my simple faith." In fact that is what this book is about, the encouragement of people to doubt, differ, and disagree without fear or favor in our constitutional democracy. My mother possessed a sure and certain knowledge of her God that never excluded another human being nor presumed anyone without her faith to be a lesser breed. She was a believer without arrogance.

The writing has proved easier because of the encouragement at the University of Richmond of Dean David Leary and Provost Zeddie Bowen. My colleagues in the religion department—Frank Eakin, Miranda Shaw, and Ted Bergren—have provided a stimulating environment and good friendship. Professor Irby Brown, a partner in so many academic endeavors, has constantly sharpened my sense of humor. I owe a continued debt to my advisor and mentor at Princeton University, Horton Davies. Additionally, through his commitment to academic freedom and integrity, Professor John Gager, also of Princeton, has been a recent reminder of the quality of that great institution.

Nothing in my career has been without encouragement and help from my family. We hold a set of common values concerning personal freedom and education that make lively discussions inevitable and frequent. This endeavor, like all those that have gone before, owes the most to my wife, Norma. She has been the sounding board for all the ideas and planning for this volume. Our sons Bob and John have both encouraged and critiqued my work. Their insights into the children they teach along with the thoughts of our daughters-in-law, Vickie and Pam, both teachers as well, have affected my thinking about the school children who are the objects of all the debate over classroom prayer.

Introduction

Congress shall make no law respecting an establishment of
religion, or prohibiting the free exercise thereof; . . .

While the adoption of these sixteen words by the Congress in
1789 was certainly fraught with considerable conflict, nothing
in the records provides an unmistakable guide to the nuances
that modern scholars have applied to the early debates about
them. We have available a brief record of House discussions of
what became the first freedom of the First Amendment. There
is little more than conjecture upon which to depend when examining the product of Senate debate, for that body kept almost
no records for later public consumption.

The extant material is examined here in order to shed as
much light as possible upon congressional intentions but, as James
Madison observed concerning the Constitutional Convention of
1787, even possessing full records of debates does not justify
slavish adherence to the opinions generated at the time. Of equal
importance were the debates that took place state by state over

ratification. Perhaps of even greater significance may be the living Constitution in relation to each successive generation. Such a perspective would provide a peaceful alternative to Jefferson's oft-noted suggestion that a revolution might be appropriate for a democracy in every generation. It would conform to Madison's sentiment that "the advice nearest to my heart and deepest in my convictions is that the Union of the States be cherished and perpetuated."[1]

Early in the history of the nation it became clear that the keeper of the union and its Constitution would be the Supreme Court. Neither Congress nor the president could manifest the integrity and distance required to maintain the document. Illustrative of just that point is an obscure essay honoring Chief Justice John Marshall to be found in *The Evangelical Inquirer* for the year 1827. Forty years after the Constitutional Convention the newspaper published for its Baptist constituents in Virginia the following sentiment:

> Such has been the confidence of a thinking people in the ability and integrity of their highest Court, that potent States and turbulent parties, have again and again acquiesced in decisions irritating to their pride and repugnant to their local interest— decisions and events pregnant with political benefit to great and polished communities, by exhibiting the efficacy of moral influence enthroned upon the ruins of the *ultima ratio regum*, which has enslaved mankind. The moral influence of Washington's unparalleled character during his energetic and momentous life, proved the sheet anchor of our fluctuating vessel of state. Since the loss of the utility of that immense counterpoise to faction, it is in vain for superficial leaders to deny, that such *needful weight in this vast confederacy, has been chiefly supplied by the wisdom of the decrees of the Supreme Court of the United States.* And the truth of this asseveration, which

will be developed and demonstrated by historians of the next century, affords even now the best eulogy of our Chief Justice.[2]

Sentiments such as these should remind current interpreters that while a careful analysis of events producing the First Amendment are critically important, they provide, at best, a backdrop for discussion and debate. Sifting through the correspondence of the founders is a stimulating historical exercise. Indeed, using the past as prologue neither diminishes history nor endangers the principles that affected the character of the new nation. However, such study may become debilitating when one slavishly seeks actions and quotations that enhance a particular bias. In short, rigid adherence to some notion of "original intent" will frequently lead authoritarians to find ways to worship dead radicals.

In this study our chief constitutional concern will be the First Amendment. As one looks back to the founders it is imperative to recall that the amendment acquired new character and meaning the very moment it was freed from the restrictive phrase "Congress shall make no law." Precedent and *stare decisis* have taken the Amendment far from its moorings in the Senate secret debates. Through what is termed "incorporation," an emerging pluralistic society came to possess an inheritance unimagined either by Congress or the ratifying states.

The focus of this volume is the Congress and its relation to the religion clauses of the First Amendment, manifest in interactions with presidents and justices in the past forty years over the subject of prayer in the public schools. Once we have examined Madison as he and his colleagues applied free exercise and nonestablishment to their own day, our attention will shift to the interim nineteenth century, characterized by what Digby Baltzell labelled the "Protestant Establishment."[3] This history will lay the foundation for a consideration of the interplay of Court, president, and Congress in the twentieth century. We will *not* be asking, "What would Madison do if he were alive today?" Rather we will inquire as to why he acted and wrote as he did during his long life of eighty-five years and how that may assist in a rational response to current conflicts.

There is no conclusion possible for this study. The final chapter is speculative. Yet as we focus on the thirty-year debate over prayer in public schools from *Engel* to *Weisman*, with Congressional documents as our chief text, it is hoped that this examination of the sources may prove a reliable guide to reasoned exchanges that will be instructive as new battle lines are drawn in the ongoing controversy over the First Amendment's establishment clause.

One of the most consistent voices for freedom of mind and body in this century has been Henry Steele Commager. As he began to draw the curtains on his continuing illustrious career he was given to eloquence in a 1983 address to a Washington gathering honoring James Madison. It was the *character* of the founders that captured Commager's imagination. He wrote of virtue that encompassed the likes of Hamilton, Jefferson, Paine, Washington, Adams, and Madison. America relied, he wrote,

> on reason as well as on faith, embraced mankind rather than the individual, and was ever conscious of the claims of posterity—a word that has all but disappeared from our vocabulary today. It did not reject Jesus or the Gospels but took from these—as with Jefferson's compilation of the life and morals of Jesus—what was universally valid. Its testaments, moral, philosophical, or political, celebrated virtue, happiness, equality in the sight of God and the law, justice, and life here rather

than hereafter. It believed in one form of immortality—the immortality of fame—which was the spur: "Take care of me when I am dead," Jefferson wrote Madison; it was in a sense the *cri de coeur* of their generation.[4]

In his last letter to Jefferson, dated February 24, 1826, Madison put it directly: "We cannot be deprived of the happy consciousness of the pure devotion to the public good with which we discharged the trusts committed to us."[5] Having been witness to the political realities of 1992 one is reminded of how distant our present political "operations" are from that spirit of leadership.

Notes

1. Irving Brant, *James Madison: Commander in Chief*, vol. 6 (New York: The Bobbs-Merril Co., 1961), p. 530.
2. Quoted from "Art. VIII.—Biographical. *Chief Justice Marshall.*" *The Evangelical Inquirer* 1, no. 12 (Sept. 1827): 382–84. The essay was followed by the note, *Colvin's Mess.*, suggesting the original source of the sentiments espoused by the Virginia editor. Marshall died in 1835 after 34 years as Chief Justice.
3. E. Digby Baltzell, *The Protestant Establishment: Aristocracy and Caste in America* (New Haven: Yale University Press, 1987).
4. Henry Steele Commager, "Take Care of Me When I am Dead," in *James Madison on Religious Liberty*, Robert S. Alley, ed. (Buffalo, N.Y.: Prometheus Books, 1985), p. 332.
5. Gaillard Hunt, *The Writings of James Madison*, vol. 9, 1819–36 (New York: G. P. Putnam's Sons, 1910), p. 245.

1

The Architect of the Religion Clauses:
James Madison

Little in the early history of British colonial settlement of North America seemed a harbinger for religious freedom in the "new world." Even as James I persecuted English citizens for their departure from Anglican orthodoxy, the settlers of Jamestown in 1607 established the Church of England in the colony of Virginia. So thoroughly did that establishment become ingrained in Virginia that in the 1750s, a century and a half later, Presbyterians found themselves objects of restrictive colonial action. The next two English colonies brought variations of religious establishment, more lenient in Plymouth (Separatists), more restrictive in Massachusetts (Puritans). Another form of establishment emerged in Maryland, broader in conception but still Christian. The liberal spirit of New Jersey and Pennsylvania maintained toleration as the operating principle; however this was limited as suggested by William Penn's *Frame of Government*. It provided full rights to all citizens "who profess in Jesus Christ."

Those middle colonies were quite consistent with the ideas espoused by John Locke in his *Letters of Toleration*. He supported a national church comprehensive in creed. As Locke scholar A. C. Fraser observed, "He had no objection to a national establishment of religion, provided that it was comprehensive enough, and was really the nation organized to promote goodness; not to protect the metaphysical subtleties of sectarian theologians. The recall of the national religion to the simplicity of the gospels would, he hoped, make toleration of nonconformists unnecessary, as few would, he hoped, remain."[1] Locke refused any idea of toleration for atheists because "the taking away of God dissolves all."

Locke's views should not be confused, though they almost invariably are, with "free exercise of religion," a concept espoused in seventeenth-century America only in Rhode Island by the likes of Roger Williams and John Clarke. The latter wrote that Rhode Island wished "to be permitted to hold forth in a lively experiment that a flourishing civil state may stand, yea, and that among English spirits, with a full liberty of religious concernments."[2]

Williams based his endorsement of religious freedom on his Christian theology. He believed that coercion in matters of belief was offensive to God and that such conversions were neither efficacious nor in the spirit of Christ. He insisted that there was a proper distinction between sacred and secular. Further, he believed that coercion by the state should only be in the arena of the secular. After Williams's death in 1681, Rhode Island reverted to a form of Protestant establishment similar to its neighbors.

In 1689 England came to terms with its Protestant religious diversity via William and Mary and the Act of Toleration. England resolved its most dangerous conflicts with a mild establishment of Anglicanism and broad tolerance of all other Protestants. But because the confrontations in England involved a single central government to which all religious believers were loyal, the resolution of 1689, resulting from a century and a half of struggle, persecution, war and negotiation focused upon a single solution— establishment. In contrast, each of the colonies became an administrative entity with, in each instance, an established religion of some kind. Whether narrowly Anglican or Puritan, or more broadly tolerant in the Separatist or Quaker mold, the same type of struggle that took place in a united England emerged thirteen times over in the colonies with quite different results from Massachusetts to Virginia to Maryland to Pennsylvania. Thus the Parliament's "Act of Toleration" meant a completely different thing in New Jersey than it did in eighteenth-century Virginia. There was never "an" establishment common to all colonies.

By the second decade of the eighteenth century religious fervor among Presbyterians in the middle colonies created what has come to be known as the Great Awakening. It spread first north to New England where it fell on hard soil, and then to the South, a far more receptive area. The Awakening would create a unique American religious tradition of the Protestant persuasion, ultimately extremely loyal to the cause of revolution. The movement was a significant influence in the spread of toleration among the colonies, at least the tolerance of various Protestant alternatives. Nevertheless, ingrained in the Awakening movement was the acceptance of religious establishment which at it's most enlightened, was along the lines defined by Locke. As commerce and communication among the colonies became more and more the rule, the bonds among the white, English Protestants of whatever theology became stronger than any that persisted in relation to the mother country.

One of the first evidences of theology in service to the emerging independent governments of the colonies came in the French and Indian War. Haranguing his parishioners with antipapal sentiments and Protestant pride, the Rev. Mr. Samuel Davies became one of the best recruiting officers for the militia in Virginia. A Presbyterian, Davies lived in his adopted colony for twelve years (1747–59). He respected the established Anglican Church, but he insisted that Virginia law be made consistent with the Parliament's Act of Toleration. He objected to colonial officials arbitrarily denying him and his colleagues licenses to preach. His vision and the growing variety of Protestants in all the colonies made his struggle a foregone success. By the time he left Virginia in 1759 Protestant toleration had been achieved in the most rigid of the thirteen colonies.

By the early 1760s Baptists moved in ever larger numbers into Virginia. One segment of that sect rejected the authority of the state to issue licenses, thereby creating a bitter struggle against them by colonial officials.[3] A goodly number of the sect's clergy were imprisoned in that decade and the next for their refusal to obtain licenses before preaching. There existed no body of political thought capable of cutting through this conflict with advanced principles that would extend beyond traditional toleration.

It was at this point in history that James Madison entered the picture. As public servant, legislator, and confidant of other giants of the early days of the Republic, Madison was the consummate American citizen. None has shone more brightly before or since.

Examining the already extensive new edition (nineteen volumes) of James Madison's *Papers* that take us only to 1801,[4] the range of his interests is remarkable and the concentration on the art of government is most stunning. A very small portion of the Madison material relates to freedom of religion, but it was the subject that first excited him to political action and to which he returned in his last years with a ringing endorsement of the American experiment in religious freedom.

Education without a Cause

Ralph Ketcham, in an excellent biography of James Madison, comments, "When Madison went to the middle colonies and to the Presbyterian stronghold at Princeton [The College of New Jersey], he placed himself at the center of the English dissenting tradition in North America."[5] But Madison did not gain from that exposure explicit rejection of all forms of establishment. It was his genius that moved him from those early influences supporting a liberal form of toleration to a grander concept, religious liberty.

When, in 1772, Madison returned home to Montpelier he entered into correspondence with his close friend, William Bradford of Philadelphia. Perusal of this material reveals some interesting facts. In November 1772 Madison appeared despondent, anticipating an early death. A year later, in September, he was less introspective and offered serious advice to his friend about choosing a profession. On December 1, 1773, Madison learned that Bradford had chosen the law. At this point we come upon Madison's first reference to a serious political interest. He asked Bradford for a draft of the Pennsylvania constitution, "particularly the extent of your religious Toleration." One can feel Madison come alive as he asks, "Is an Ecclesiastical Establishment absolutely necessary to support civil society in a supreme Government? And how far is it hurtful to a dependent State?" Something was at work on the young man. On January 24, 1774, he wrote again to Bradford, "Ecclesiastical Establishments tend to great ignorance and Corruption all of which facilitate the Execution of mischievous Projects." He spoke of poverty and political corruption before the following moving observation:

This is bad enough. But It is not the worst I have to tell you. That diabolical Hell conceived principle of persecution rages among some and to their eternal Infamy the Clergy can furnish their quota of Imps for such business. This vexes me the most of any thing whatever. There are at this time in the adjacent County not less than 5 or 6 well meaning men in close Goal for publishing their religious Sentiments which in the main are very orthodox. I have neither patience to hear talk or think any thing relative to this matter, for I have squabbled and scolded, abused and ridiculed so long about it, to so little purpose that I am without common patience. So I leave you to pity me and pray for Liberty of Conscience [to revive among us].[6]

By April 1774 Madison was writing about the "rights of conscience."

Madison's vexation appears to have raised him from his lethargy and eliminated his concerns over an early death. He had a cause that ignited him. And in two consecutive letters we find him moving from tentative commitment through a theory of toleration to his basic, lifelong espousal of the principle of liberty of conscience. There is little doubt that Madison, in the few months between the two letters to his friend, had answered his own question about establishment and moved to a new level beyond toleration.

The word toleration has a sweet ring in modern America. It denotes a sense of justice and respect for differing views. We urge our children to retain that natural spirit of tolerance in mind and action that characterizes five-year-old girls and boys. But for a state to be tolerant is quite another matter. Here the implication is that the state has the right to enforce tyranny and exercises tolerance out of its largesse. Tom Paine would later characterize toleration as despotism. Madison agreed. In 1785 he put his concerns in classic form: "Who does not see that the same authority which can establish Christianity, in exclusion of all other Religions, may establish with the same ease any particular sect of Christians, in exclusion of all other Sects?" (*Memorial and Remonstrance*) As he expressed it in an auto-biographical note in 1832, Madison contended for freedom of conscience as a natural and absolute right. Toleration presumed a state prerogative that, for Madison, did not exist. The right to tolerate religion presumes the right to persecute it. Madison had no hesitation in describing the ideal relationship between church and state: separation. He wrote in 1832 about Jefferson's Bill for Establishing Religious Freedom in Virginia.

> Here the separation between the authority of human laws, and the natural rights of Man excepted from the grant on which all political authority is founded, is traced as distinctly as words can admit, and the limits to this authority established with as much solemnity as the forms of legislation can express.[7]

It is fair then to surmise that the young Madison first felt his intense, lifelong commitment to freedom focusing on political action as he observed the persecution by his own government of those ministers in close jail. Whatever influences sent him to the Virginia Convention two years later, the emotional reactions to the abuse of the dissenters in 1774 was a critically significant factor.

The Virginia Declaration of Rights

In May 1776 Madison was elected to the Revolutionary Convention in Virginia. He was selected to serve on a committee

to compose a declaration of rights for the new government. George
Mason, an elder statesman in Virginia, proposed an article about
religion that read, "All men should enjoy the fullest toleration
in the exercise of religion." Madison suggested replacing the word
"toleration." He already appeared to view the term as an "invidious
concept." He proposed to substitute, "All men are equally entitled
to the free exercise of religion." Historian George Bancroft would
describe that phrase as "the first achievement of the wisest civilian
in Virginia."

A little-noted suggestion by Madison respecting the Declaration of Rights, included with his move to insert free exercise, was
the affirmation that "Unless under colour of religion, the preservation of equal liberty and the existence of the State be manifestly
endangered."[8] This may be the clearest indication of Madison's
dual fear of establishment. Not only was he concerned over the
loss of religious freedom, but he was equally concerned over the
threat to a democratic state posed by religious establishment.

The Virginia Struggle after the Revolution

The all-consuming character of the war with Britain left little
time to make further changes in the laws of Virginia. The Virginia
legislature did address the subject of religious establishment in
1778. Jefferson found himself resisting efforts to perpetuate the
traditional tie between state and church, and attempts to create
a general assessment to support Protestant churches. These
conflicts meant he was unable to have his Bill for Establishing
Religious Freedom in Virginia, written in 1777, passed during
his time in the legislature.

With the conclusion of the war Madison took his place in
the governing body of Virginia. Almost immediately he was con-

fronted with the same two threats to freedom. First, there was the renewed effort to establish the Episcopal Church in the state as the natural successor to the Anglican establishment.[9] Second, there was a General Assessment Bill that would assign tax monies to support religious education by Protestant churches, a project justified by its supporters as a means of curtailing the sin and immorality of the young people. The bill's rationale sounded the same sentiments set forth by Locke in the previous century.

In the fall of 1784 Madison knew that he could not deflect both of these pieces of legislation. Politicians were not likely to cast two votes "against God" in the same session. Madison was opposed to the established Church of England, as indicated in his letters to William Bradford in 1773. The dilemma for him in 1784 was quickly resolved in his mind. He voted for Episcopalian establishment. It passed. He then convinced his colleagues to postpone a vote on assessment until the next session in 1785. Madison believed that the assessment bill was a far more insidious form of establishment. He was convinced that it would result in an established Protestantism in eighteenth-century Virginia, combining, as it did, the interests of most Protestant religious factions. The consequence could well be a permanent condition. Writing to his father on January 6, 1785, Madison explained his decision.

> The inclosed Act for incorporating the Episcopal Church is the result of much altercation on the subject. In its original form it was wholly inadmissable. In its present form into which it has been trimmed, I assented to it with reluctance at the time, and with dissatisfaction on review of it. . . . I consider the passage of this Act however as having been so far useful as to have parried for the present the Gen!. Assesst. which would otherwise have certainly been saddled upon us: & If it be

> unpopular among the laity it will be soon repealed, and will
> be a standing lesson to them of the danger of referring religious
> matters to the legislature.[10]

The reason for Madison's choice in the Fall of 1784 is clear
enough, confirming as it did his consistent view that the state
had most to fear from the "tyranny of the majority." He was
certain that Presbyterians and Baptists would not long tolerate
the preeminent position of the Episcopal Church. He was correct.
By the close of the century it had been stripped not only of its
established status, but of its land holdings, obtained in prerevolutionary times. For Madison the great danger was establishment
of a coalition of Protestant groups that would be impervious to
arguments against it. He foresaw a classic case of majority tyranny relegating minority religious views to a "tolerated" status.

Madison now faced two tasks. He had to enlist public opposition to the assessment bill and he had to deal with the oratory
of his chief adversary, Patrick Henry. Commenting upon Henry,
Jefferson wrote his friend Madison in December 1784: "What we
have to do I think is devoutly to pray for his death, in the meantime
to keep alive the idea that the present is but an ordinance and
to prepare the minds of the young men. I am glad the Episcopalians
have again shewn their teeth & fangs. The dissenters had almost
forgotten them."[11] Rather than take Jefferson's religious option
concerning Henry, Madison used, as Ralph Ketcham wryly notes,
the secular humanist alternative and helped elect Henry as governor, thereby silencing his silver tongue.

After the General Assembly adjourned, having authorized
distribution of the assessment bill to the voters, in the spring
Madison was persuaded by friends to write a document attacking
it. The result was a severe critique in the form of a petition
to the General Assembly distributed as a broadside by Madison

to his fellow Virginians. That *Memorial and Remonstrance* became the classic statement for religious freedom in North America (see Appendix A).

Newly elected delegates, his *Memorial,* and a massive petition drive by dissenters in the state gave Madison his victory over the assessment bill without ever having to argue in the Assembly against it. He chose that season to champion Jefferson's Bill to Establish Religious Freedom in Virginia and, with some significant alterations of the original wording in the prologue,[12] the bill became law on January 19, 1786. As predicted by Madison, Episcopal establishment was repealed shortly thereafter. Meanwhile Madison was off to Philadelphia to help fashion a new constitution.

The Philadelphia Convention of 1787

Little information is forthcoming from examination of Madison's notes on the Constitutional Convention concerning the two occasions when religion became an issue before that assemblage. On June 28 Benjamin Franklin addressed his colleagues:

> The small progress we have made after 4 or five weeks . . . is methinks a melancholy proof of the imperfection of the Human Understanding. . . . how has it happened, Sir, that we have not hitherto once thought of humbly applying to the Father of lights to illuminate our understandings?[13]

Franklin went on to credit God for victory over Great Britain and asked whether "we imagine we no longer need his assistance?" He concluded:

I have lived, Sir, a long time, and the longer I live, the more convincing proofs I see of this truth—that God Governs in the affairs of men. . . . I therefore beg leave to move—that henceforth prayers imploring the assistance of Heaven, and its blessings on our deliberations, be held in this Assembly every morning before we proceed to business, and that one or more of the Clergy of this City be requested to officiate in that Service.

Madison made no indication that he himself entered the debate, noting only, "Mr. Hamilton and several others expressed their apprehensions that however proper such a resolution might have been at the beginning" it could now lead "the public to believe that the embarrassments and dissensions within the Convention, had suggested this measure." And of course it was precisely that thought that had prompted Franklin's words. Hugh Williamson of North Carolina suggested the omission of prayer was due to a lack of funds. Madison concluded, "After several unsuccessful attempts for silently postponing the matter by adjourning the adjournment was at length carried, without any vote on the motion." Seemingly an embarrassing interlude followed when the delegates, anxious not to offend the elder statesman, fumbled about until they just dispersed. The idea for prayer never resurfaced.

This is a revealing episode. Franklin clearly believed that prayer would secure success in their deliberations. His point was never addressed as those who spoke all dealt with public opinion, suggesting that for most of the men public prayer was a form without substantial benefit other than good feelings and appearances. Hamilton and others construed the Franklin suggestions, under other circumstances, as having good public relations value to the extent that it might haved conveyed a positive message to the electorate. But the efficacy of prayer was not at issue for the leaders in Philadelphia. These were men satisfied that their creator had endowed them with minds with which to think. Their religious sentiments were consistently expressed in an enlightened humanism that respected the image of the deity that many felt resided in the human mind. At most, prayer was a habit of affirmation of that humanism, little more. So much for Franklin's views on the God of history.

Respecting Article VI Madison's notes provide no clue as to the reasoning behind the religious test provision. Charles Pinckney of South Carolina submitted a set of propositions on August 20. Among them was: "No religious test or qualification shall ever be annexed to any oath of office under the authority of the U.S." This was referred to the Committee of detail without debate or consideration. On August 30 Pinckney moved to add to what was to become Article VI, "but no religious test shall ever be required as a qualification to any office or public trust under the authority of the U. States." Roger Sherman of Connecticut "thought it unnecessary, the prevailing liberality being a sufficient security against such tests." Governor Morris of Pennsylvania joined in support of the amendment. The motion was then agreed to. In a letter to Jefferson in 1788 Madison noted reservations among some about this provision. "One of the objections in New England was that the Constitution by prohibiting religious tests opened the door for Jews, Turks and infidels."

Notes

1. Alexander Campbell Fraser, "John Locke," in *The Encyclopedia Britannica*, 11th ed. (1911), vol. 16, p. 846.

2. Appleton's *Cyclopedia of American Biography*, vol. 1, p. 634.

See Anson Phelps Stokes and Leo Pfeffer, *Church and State in the United States* (New York: Harper and Row, 1964), p. 18.

3. It is interesting that President Clinton took the Sunday before his inauguration to meet with the congregation of the Culpeper Baptist Church, located in the town where several preachers were imprisoned.

4. One caveat is necessary. The *Presidential Series* was inaugurated in 1984: Robert Rutland, Thomas A. Mason, et al., eds., *The Papers of James Madison, Presidential Series* (Charlottesville: University Press of Virginia, 1984ff.). The best source for the correspondence extending through 1836 remains Gaillard Hunt, ed., *The Writings of James Madison* (New York: G. P. Putnam's Sons, 1900), 9 vols.

5. Ralph Ketcham, *James Madison* (Charlottesville: University Press of Virginia, 1990), p. 38.

6. "Letter to William Bradford from James Madison, January 24, 1774," in William T. Hutchinson and William M. E. Rachal, eds., *The Papers of James Madison*, vol. 1 (University of Chicago Press, 1962), p. 106. It is not made clear in this correspondence exactly what was taking place in Madison's own county of Orange, but later references make it clear that he was occupied with the cause of freedom in Orange. The editors confirm my assessment about Madison's motivation. They note, "Apparently it was religious issues, more than tax and trade regulation disputes with England, which were rapidly luring JM away from his beloved studies and arousing his interest in contemporary politics" (see note 9 on page 106).

7. In this version of his autobiography, *Detached Memoranda*, edited by Elizabeth Fleet in *The William and Mary Quarterly*, 1946, p. 554, Madison expanded on several concerns having to do with religion and state, including chaplains and presidential proclamations.

8. See Gaillard Hunt, ed., *The Writings of James Madison* (New York: G. P. Putnam's Sons, 1900), vol. 1, p. 41.

9. In October 1776 the laws of Virginia were amended to read: "That all and every act of parliament, by whatever title known or distinguished, which renders criminal the maintaining any opinions in matters of religion, forbearing to repair to church, or the exercising

any mode of worship whatsoever, or which prescribes punishments for the same, shall henceforth be of no validity or force within this commonwealth." Further it was agreed, "That all dissenters, of whatever denomination, from the said church, shall, from and after the passing of this act, be totally free and exempt from all levies, taxes, and impositions whatever, towards supporting and maintaining the said church, as it now is or hereafter may be established, and its ministers." The result was retaining a skeleton of establishment with no funding or power of enforcement. This same act anticipated the debates of 1784 with another provision. "And whereas great variety of opinions hath arisen, touching the propriety of a general assessment, or whether every religious society should be left to voluntary contributions for the support and maintenance of the several ministers and teachers of the gospel who are of different persuasions and denominations, and this difference of sentiments cannot now be well accommodated, so that it is thought most prudent to defer this matter to the discussion and final determination of a future assembly, when the opinions of the country in general may be better known: To the end, therefore, that so important a subject may in no sort be prejudged, *Be it enacted, by the authority aforesaid,* That nothing in this act contained shall be construed to affect or influence the said question of a general assessment, or voluntary contribution, in any respect whatever." The Assembly went on to suspend state payment of salaries for establishment ministers. This suspension remained in place through annual reaffirmation throughout the Revolution. See William Waller Hening, *The Statutes at Large; A Collection of all the Laws of Virginia,* vol. 9 (Richmond: J. & G. Cochran, 1821), pp. 164–66.

    10. "Letter from James Madison, Jr., to James Madison, Sr., January 6, 1785," in Robert Rutland and William M. E. Rachal, eds., *The Papers of James Madison,* vol. 8 (Chicago: University of Chicago Press, 1973), p. 217.

    11. Unless otherwise noted, all correspondence quoted can be found in *The Papers of James Madison,* currently being published by the University Press of Virginia now under the editorship of David B.

Mattern. This is a continuation of volumes noted in note 10 above. The sources are recorded in chronological order in that multivolume project.

12. The changes were not without significance. Jefferson had originally included the following phrases in Section I: (a) "well aware that the opinions and belief of men depend not on their own will, but follow involuntarily the evidence proposed to their minds"; (b) "manifested his supreme will that free it [the mind] shall remain by making it altogether insusceptible of restraint"; (c) "but to extend it [religion] by its influence on reason alone"; (d) "and abhors"; (e) "that the opinions of men are not the object of civil government, nor under its jurisdiction." Each omission clearly marks out a division between the deistic, rationalist Jeffersonian principles and the more orthodox view of traditional churchmen in Virginia. Madison realized that only with the deletions could the bill be approved and hoped Jefferson would understand. Writing to his friend on January 21, 1786, he noted: "The preamble was sent up again from the H. of D. with one or two verbal alterations. As an amendment to these the Senate sent down a few others; which as they did not affect the substance though they somewhat defaced the composition, it was thought better to agree to than to run further risks, especially as it was getting late in the Session and the House growing thin. The enacting clauses past without a single alteration, and I flatter myself have in this Country extinguished for ever the ambitious hope of making laws for the human mind."

13. James Madison, *The Debates in the Federal Convention of 1787* (Buffalo, N.Y.: Prometheus Books, 1987), vol 1, pp. 181–82. As the Congress became involved in responding to school prayer decisions of the Supreme Court, many a witness quoted Franklin in order to prove how dependent on prayer the nation had been at its inception. One of them created a mythological conclusion to the discussion on prayer in Philadelphia. Sen. A. Willis Robertson of Virginia, out of thin air asserted that thereafter the Constitutional Convention opened every session with prayer.

2

Constitutional Ratification and a Bill of Rights: The Virginia Experience

Road to the Richmond Ratification Convention, 1788

When the Constitutional Convention concluded in Philadelphia James Madison, as a member of Congress under the Articles of Confederation, returned to New York, where he assisted in the passage of the necessary resolutions that would send the newly written document to the states for ratification. The task was not altogether easy. Madison argued against efforts to have the Congress amend the Constitution. Some members of Congress "urged the expediency of sending out the plan with amendments, & proposed a number of them corresponding with the objections of Col. Mason. This experiment had still less effect. In order however to obtain unanimity it was necessary to couch the resolution in very moderate terms."[1]

As Madison revealed in that same letter, he had serious misgivings about the likely success of the new constitution. He was troubled because the federal government lacked the power to veto state laws. He feared the "virus of tyranny," which he felt was most rampant at the state level. He wrote, "A check on the States appears to me necessary 1. to prevent encroachments on the General authority. 2. to prevent instability and injustice in the legislation of the States." Elaborating on this theme, Madison offered an extensive commentary on the threat to minority sects from the religious enthusiasm of the majority.

The inefficacy of this restraint on individuals is well known. The conduct of every popular Assembly, acting on oath, the strongest of religious ties, shews that individuals join without remorse in acts agst. which their consciences would revolt, if proposed to them separately in their closets. When Indeed Religion is kindled into enthusiasm, its force like that of other passions is increased by the sympathy of a multitude. But enthusiasm is only a temporary state of Religion, and whilst it lasts will hardly be seen with pleasure at the helm. Even in its coolest state, it has been much oftener a motive to oppression than a restraint from it. If then there must be different interests and parties in Society; and a majority when united by a common interest or passion can not be restrained from oppressing the minority, what remedy can be found in a republican Government, where the majority must ultimately decide, but that of giving such an extent to its sphere, that no common interest or passion will be likely to unite a majority of the whole number in an unjust pursuit. In a large Society, the people are broken into so many interests and parties, that a common sentiment is less likely to be felt, and the requisite concert less likely to be formed, by a majority of the whole. The same security seems requisite for the civil as for the religious rights of individuals. If the same sect form a majority and have the power, other sects will be sure to be depressed. Divide et impera, the reprobated axiom of tyranny, is under certain qualifications, the only policy, by which a republic can be administered on just principles. . . . The General Government would hold a pretty even balance between the parties of particular States, and be at the same time sufficiently restrained by its dependence on the community, from betraying its general interests.[2]

It was this same concern that led Madison in 1789, unsuccessfully, to place in the Bill of Rights the provision that the secured rights applied to state law as well as to laws made by Congress.

Having been one of the fifty-five men to prepare the Constitution in Philadelphia, having argued for its passage through the Congress, and along with his colleagues Hamilton and Jay, having written extensively in defense of the Constitution in his remarkable contributions to the *Federalist Papers*, Madison was dubious about being selected a delegate to the Richmond Convention set to consider ratification in June 1788. However, prior to the first ratification by Delaware on December 2, 1787, Madison had declared his reluctant intention to stand for election to the Virginia Convention. In a November 8, 1787, letter to his brother, Ambrose, he wrote:

Having mislaid your last favor, I can not acknowledge it by reference to its date. It contained two requests, . . . the other to my being a candidate in Orange for the Convention. . . . In answer to the second point, I am to observe that it was not my wish to have followed the Act of the General Convention into the Convention of the States; supposing that it would be as well that the final decision thereon should proceed from men who had no hand preparing and proposing it. As I find however that in all the States the members of the Genl. Convention are becoming members of the State Conventions, as I have been applied to on the subject by sundry very respectable friends, as I have reason to believe that many objections in Virginia proceed from a misconception of the plan, or of the causes which produced the objectionable parts of it; and as my attendance at Philadelphia, may enable me to contribute some explanations and information which may be of use, I shall not decline the representation of the County if I should be honoured with its appointment. You may let this be known in such way as my father & yourself may judge best. I shall be glad to hear from [you] on the subject, and to know what competition there will probably be and by whom.[3]

At least one letter survives that demonstrates the early concern by his Virginia friends that Madison seek to attend the Richmond Convention set for June 1, 1788. On October 25, 1787, the Virginia Assembly set that date. On November 2 Archibald Stuart wrote, "It is generally considered necessary that you should be of the Convention, not only that the Constitution may be adopted but with as much unanimity as possible. For gods sake do not disappoint the Anxious expectations of yr friends & let me add of yr Country."[4] A couple of months later Edmund Pendleton expressed similar feelings in a letter of January 29, 1788. He urged Madison to be a delegate to the ratification convention. He stated, "But too much of myself: it is much more important that you should be there, and wish for that reason that you could be in your County some time before the day, lest some designing men may endeavour to avail themselves of yr. Absence."[5]

On November 22 Madison's famous *Federalist* no. 10 appeared in the New York *Daily Advertiser*. On January 11 Madison took up his pen again with no. 37 and over the next six weeks wrote some twenty-two essays. Toward the end of that period he penned a letter to George Washington detailing his plans:

I have given notice to my friends in Orange that the County may command my services in the Convention if it pleases. I can say with great truth however that in this overture I sacrifice every private inclination to considerations not of a selfish nature. I foresee that the undertaking will involve me in very laborious and irksome discussions; that public opposition to several very respectable characters whose esteem and friendship I greatly prize may unintentionally endanger the subsisting connection; and that disagreeable misconstructions, of which samples have been already given, may be the fruit of those exertions which fidelity will impose. But I have made up my determination on the subject; and if I am informed that my presence at the election in the County be indispensable, shall submit to that condition also; though it is my particular wish to decline it, as well to avoid apparent solicitude on the occasion; as a journey of such length at a very unplesant season.[6]

On the same day he made it clear in a letter to Jefferson that he had already determined to travel to Virginia. "By letter just received from Virginia I find that I shall be under the necessity of setting out in 8 or 10 days for Virginia." Undoubtedly this is a reference to a letter of February 17 from James Gordon stating, "It is incumbent on you with out delay, to repair to this state."[7]

By mid-February six states, including Pennsylvania, New Jersey and Massachusetts had ratified the Constitution. And before Virginia ratified on June 25 the requisite nine states had approved the document. Nevertheless, Hamilton and Madison were aware that without New York and Virginia the new union would be hopelessly flawed.

So Madison departed New York on his critically important mission March 3 or 4, just after writing to Washington that he had promised himself "the pleasure of taking Mount Vernon in the way." He stopped at Mount Vernon on March 18 and 19 and departed on the morning of March 20, arriving in Fredericks-burg some time on March 21. There he was probably given a letter from a Joseph Spencer that had been addressed to Madison in the care of F. Maury. The identity of Spencer is not known and there is no written evidence that the letter was actually delivered on March 21. All that is known for certain is that Madison eventually received the letter and recorded it as being dated February 26, 1788.

The content of the Spencer letter was alarmist, a sentiment that does not seem extreme in light of Madison's letter to Eliza House Trist on March 25. Spencer stated that the Constitution had enemies in Orange. He noted that Madison's opponent in the upcoming March 24 election, Thomas "Barber," had as friends "in a general way the Baptus's," and that "the Prechers of that Society are much alrm'd fearing Religious liberty is not Suffi-ciently secur'd they pretend to other objections but that I think is the principle objection."[8] Spencer identified John Leland, a Baptist preacher in Orange, as the most significant leader of this faction. Spencer urged Madison "as Mr. Leeland Lyes in your Way home from Fredericksburg to Orange would advise you'l call on him & Spend a few Howers in his Company" in order to persuade Leland to support the Constitution. It is not clear when Madison left Fredericksburg, possibly late in the day on the 21st. Records reveal that Madison was expected for dinner at the home of his friend Maj. Moore. Madison failed to arrive before other guests departed. A March 23 diary entry for one of the guests, Francis Taylor, states, "Heard that Col. Madison got to Majr. Moores last night and proceeded today to his fathers."[9] In the letter to Eliza Trist dated March 25 Madison informed her, "The badness of the roads & some other delays retarded the completion of my journey till the day before yesterday [March 23]." Madison was home in Montpelier the day before the election.

The Trist letter provides the best account of the events on election day, March 24.

> I had the satisfaction to find all my friends well on my arrival; and the chagrin to find the County filled with the most absurd and groundless prejudices against the federal Constitution. I was therefore obliged at the election which succeeded the day of my arrival to mount for the first time in my life, the rostrum before a large body of the people, and to launch into a harangue of some length in the open air and on a very windy day. What the effect might be I cannot say, but either from that experiment or the exertion of the federalists or perhaps both, the misconceptions of the Government were so far corrected that two federalists one of them myself were electd by a majority of nearly 4 to one. [Madison—202, James Gordon—187, Thomas Barbour—56, Charles Porter—34] It is very probable that a very different event would have taken place as to myself if the efforts of my friends had not been seconded by my presence.[10]

Obviously at least one person cast a single ballot and at least 240 persons voted. The maximum number that could have voted, had all persons voted only for a single candidate, would have been 479. Reason suggests a number little in excess of the 240 figure.

Madison credits his friends and his speech on March 24 for the voting results. There is absolutely no evidence from Madison or anyone during his lifetime to suggest a meeting between him and John Leland. The first indication of such an encounter was made by John Barbour in a eulogy for Madison delivered on July 18, 1836, forty-eight years after the election of 1788. Barbour orated that Madison's "soft and assuasive and lucid elocution changed two ministers of the Gospel of the Baptist Church on the day preceding the election and that conversation carried him to the Convention. The celebrated John Leland was one of them." Probably based upon the Barbour allusion, the editors of the Madison papers noted in a footnote, "Although accounts of JM's famous meeting with Leland are fanciful, the tradition is strong that such a meeting did in fact occur, probably on 22 Mar."[11]

Clearly, the record supports the fact that Baptist endorsements of the Constitution were significant in its ratification in Virginia. It was one of many factors. It does no honor to a denomination devoted to religious freedom to exaggerate the events; it merely deflects from a serious consideration of what Baptists did indeed contribute. It is therefore somewhat puzzling to find the eminent scholar and Madison biographer Ralph Ketcham asserting, as if documented, such a meeting between Leland and Madison. Ketcham wrote, without cited evidence in support, "On his way from Fredericksburg to Orange, with the election now but a few days away, Madison stopped to see the influential Baptist preacher John Leland."[12]

The Leland legend presumes that either Leland convinced Madison to support a Bill of Rights or that Madison allayed Leland's fears by guaranteeing he would support such additions to the Constitution. As was made clear by a resolution of the Virginia Baptist General Committee on March 7, 1788, the Constitution's omission of "sufficient provision for the secure enjoyment of religious liberty" was the singular concern of Leland and his colleagues. Yet Madison's first full commitment to any kind of amendments came in a letter to Alexander Hamilton on June 22, 1788. Finally, on the basis of the letter to Eliza Trist there is reason to reject as improbable any meeting at all with Leland prior to the March 24 election. This in no way diminishes Leland's important support for Madison's election. Further, Leland remained a lifelong admirer of both Madison and Jefferson, in large part because of their support for religious freedom. The most important lesson from the Baptist story is the subtext of the Patrick Henry effort to derail the Constitution by playing every prejudice to create a coalition able to scuttle the document in June of 1788. Spencer's letter noted above makes this point quite clear, as do numerous references to Henry in the Madison correspondence. Henry sought to use the Baptists, along with many other groups and individuals, in his own antifederalist interests. That he failed is a tribute to the persuasiveness of Madison both in Orange on March 24, 1788, and in Richmond three months later.

A recently recovered letter, previously cited, from Edmund Pendleton to Madison, dated January 29, 1788, focused upon unscrupulous persons manipulating the population to oppose the Constitution.

> I am told that a considerable Revolution has happened in the minds of the middle & lower Class's of people on the Subject, at which I am not at all Surprised. At first they were warmly for it, from a confidence in the wisdom & Integrity of their representatives. In the various publications and conversations on the Occasion, it is exceeding difficult, indeed impossible, to make the good people at large well Acquainted with the different forms & combinations of Power necessary to constitute Government for the protection of liberty and property: and hence they are exposed to impositions from designing men, and particularly Of those in Opposition to Government, who have the popular side, and by decrying powers as dangerous to liberty, will include indiscriminately, such as are unavoidable to good Government, with those which are really hurtful; and to this cause I attribute the change in those Sentiments, in which the people were right at first, as I believe they always are when left to their own Judgment.[13]

The Richmond Convention Convenes, June 1788

When James Madison joined his fellow delegates in Richmond he knew that much of the opposition to ratification of the Constitution centered directly upon the issue of a Bill of Rights. Often opponents of greater federal power used the Bill of Rights issue as a means to undermine the new government document. Certainly, as noted earlier, this was the case with Patrick Henry, and it seems as well to have been at work in the mind of Madison's longtime friend George Mason. Indeed, Mason, the honored architect of the Virginia Declaration of Rights in 1776, voted to reject the Constitution in the Richmond Convention. And contrary to current popular myths it was neither for love of religious freedom nor for his opposition to slavery. Mason was an antifederalist who became more and more antagonistic as the time passed in the month of June. He was concerned over questions of taxation and loss of state rights, seldom mentioning the individual rights question other than to attack the central authority of the new government. As to slavery, Mason opposed the provision that would have continued slave trade until 1808 because it would interfere with the lucrative slave breeding that took place in Virginia, serving other southern states. Indeed, delegates to the Constitutional Convention in Philadelphia from South Carolina and Georgia argued that, if the African trade were cut off, "the slaves of Virginia would rise in value, and we would be obliged to go to your markets." Further, Mason feared that the federal government did not protect slave property of those who owned slaves. Mason feared slavery could be taxed out of existence. According to Irving Brant, "Delegates jibed at Mason for being both for and against slavery."[14]

The issue in 1788 came down to whether there would be a promise of subsequent amendments, after ratification, or prior amendments. Massachusetts had chosen the former process for obvious reasons. The question before the states was the language adopted for the Constitution by the Congress. Alteration of the document would likely have no standing in law and would require, at least, that every ratifying state adopt identical language in any amendments, a highly unlikely occurrence. In fact eight states had already ratified without amendments before the matter was addressed by Virginia.

Speaking to his colleagues June 25, 1788, Madison, in response to those insisting upon amendments prior to ratification, stated, "There is no doubt they [states already having ratified] will agree to the same amendments after adoption. If we propose the constitutional amendments, I entreat gentlemen to consider the distance to which they throw the ultimate settlement, and the extreme risk of perpetual disunion."[15] Shortly thereafter the convention voted eighty ayes, eighty-eight noes on the proposal for prior or conditional amendments. On the main question of ratification the vote was eighty-nine ayes, seventy-nine noes.

In June Madison exerted all his efforts to salvage the Union. John Marshall is quoted as having observed, "Eloquence has been defined to be the art of persuasion. If it includes persuasion by convincing, Mr. Madison was the most eloquent man I ever heard." Reading the details of the debates one can understand that description. And as he worked toward a slim majority his words had to have the ring of integrity in order to hold a coalition of moderate and radical federalists. At the end a switch of four votes would have created an impasse. In retrospect the most important convincing by Madison took place in weeks before June 1 as he gently nudged Gov. Randolph toward open support of the Constitution.

Madison himself had been concerned over the Bill of Rights issue since the Philadelphia Convention. On October 24, 1787, he wrote Jefferson informing him of the content of the new Constitution and suggesting the likely outcome of a vote for ratification. Naturally, he sought to explain why only three Virginians signed the document. He noted, "Col. Mason left Philada. in an exceeding ill humour indeed. He returned to Virginia with a fixed disposition to prevent the adoption of the plan if possible. He considers the want of a Bill of Rights as a fatal objection." Madison then enumerated other objections closing with "and most of all probably to the power of regulating trade, by a majority only of each House."

Circumstances conspired to make the Bill of Rights the most obvious handle to be used by anyone opposed to the Constitution. It had the emotional tug that quickly set the population to wondering about the intentions of the new government.

Responding to Madison's letter, Jefferson wrote on December 20, "I will now add what I do not like. First the omission of a bill of rights providing clearly & without the aid of sophisms for freedom of religion, freedom of the press, . . . Let me add that a bill of rights is what the people are entitled to against every government on earth, general or particular, and what no just government should refuse or rest on inference." On February 6, 1788, Jefferson wrote again: "I am glad to hear that the new constitution is received with favor. I sincerely wish that the 9 first conventions may receive, & the 4, last reject it. The former will secure it finally; while the latter will oblige them to offer a declaration of rights in order to complete the union."

As noted previously, Madison was elected to the Virginia Ratification Convention on March 24. On April 22 he wrote to Jefferson about the Virginia situation. He was optimistic that passage was to occur, but he noted serious opposition.

The adversaries take very different grounds of opposition. Some are opposed to the substance of the plan; others to particular modifications only. Mr. H____Y is supposed to aim at disunion. Col. M____n is growing every day more bitter, and outrageous in his efforts to carry his point; and will probably in the end be thrown by the violence of his passions into the politics of Mr. H____y. The preliminary question will be whether previous alterations shall be insisted on or not?[16]

Madison was certain that conditional amendments would doom the new document and possibly union itself. Interestingly, Madison made no specific comment on a bill of rights. On July 25 he wrote to Jefferson, finally acknowledging the letters from his friend of December 20 and February 6, which had not been received until Madison's return to Virginia. Again, there was no reference to the bill of rights issue, only a brief account of the ratification. Jefferson wrote again on July 31, returning to his theme.

I sincerely rejoice at the acceptance of our new constitution by nine states. [He had not heard about the Virginia decision.] It is a good canvas, on which some strokes only want retouching. What these are, I think are sufficiently manifested by the general voice from North to South, which calls for a bill of rights. It seems pretty generally understood that this should go to Juries, Habeas corpus, Standing armies, Printing, Religion and Monopolies.

Jefferson felt that if there were no modifications to please the habits of individual states, it would be better to have unrestrained rights affirmed in all cases, "than not to do it in any." Illustrating his point he continued:

A declaration that the federal government will never restrain the presses from printing anything they please, will not take away the liability of the printers for false facts printed. The declaration that religious faith shall be unpunished, does not give impunity to criminal acts dictated by religious error. . . . I hope therefore a bill of rights will be formed to guard the people against the federal government, as they are already guarded against their state governments in most instances.[17]

Madison continued to focus on the efforts of constitutional opponents to instigate a second convention to alter the document. In an August 10 letter to Jefferson he wrote, "The great danger in the present crisis is that if another Convention should be soon assembled, it would terminate in discord, or in alterations of the federal system, which would throw back *essential* powers into the State Legislatures." Two weeks later Madison again wrote about the same subject, noting "fresh hopes and exertions to those who opposed the Constitution" in the ratification debate in North Carolina. Again, on September 21, Madison feared the impact of a circular letter from New York that "has rekindled an ardor among the opponents of the federal Constitution for an *immediate* revision of it by another General Convention." He trusted that such a move would be opposed by "those who wish for no alterations, but by others who would prefer the other mode provided in the Constitution, as most expedient at present for introducing those supplemental safeguards to liberty agst. which no objections can be raised."

So Madison became a reluctant advocate of amendments, but only through the process outlined in the Constitution itself, not through a second convention. On October 17 he wrote to Jefferson that a "constitutional declaration of the most essential rights" probably "will be added." For the first time he affirmed:

My own opinion has always been in favor of a bill of rights;
provided it be so framed as not to imply powers not meant
to be included in the enumeration. At the same time I have
never thought the omission a material defect, nor been anxious
to supply it even by *subsequent* amendment, for any other reason
than that it is anxiously desired by others.[18]

Madison went on to suggest the reasons why amendments might
still be a mistake. He noted, "A positive declaration of some of
the most essential rights could not be obtained in the requisite
latitude. I am sure that the rights of Conscience in particular,
if submitted to public definition would be narrowed much more
than they are likely ever to be by an assumed power." And he
was quite fearful of the tyranny of the majority that made such
guarantees meaningless. He wrote, "Experience proves the inefficacy of a bill of rights on those occasions when its control
is most needed. Repeated violations of these parchment barriers
have been committed by overbearing majorities in every State."

Writing in November, Jefferson agreed with Madison, "I
should deprecate with you indeed the meeting of a new convention. I hope they will adopt the mode of amendment by
Congress & and the Assemblies."

Anticipating the meeting of the new Congress, to which he
hoped to be elected, Madison wrote to Jefferson on December
8, 1788, commenting on his hopes concerning amendments. He
envisioned that the majority in that Congress would "wish the
revisal to be carried no farther than to supply additional guards
for liberty . . . and are fixed in opposition to the risk of another
Convention." He informed his friend that in creating congressional
districts Patrick Henry had seen to the association of Orange
County with areas "most likely to be swayed by the prejudices
excited agst. me." Friends urged Madison to come home to secure

a place in the new Congress. He did so in late December.

Madison undertook a campaign for election that included an important message to George Eve, minister of the Blue Run Baptist Church in Orange County, a short distance from Montpelier. Seeking Eve's support, he wrote:

> I freely own that I have never seen in the Constitution as it now stands those serious dangers which have alarmed many respectable Citizens. Accordingly whilst it remained unratified, and it was necessary to unite the States in some one plan, I opposed all previous alterations as calculated to throw the States into dangerous contentions, and to furnish the secret enemies of the Union with an opportunity of promoting its dissolution. Circumstances are now changed: The Constitution is established on the ratification of eleven States and a very great majority of the people of America; and amendments, if pursued with a proper moderation and in a proper mode, will be not only safe, but may serve the double purpose of satisfying the minds of well meaning opponents, and of providing additional guards in favour of liberty. Under this change of circumstances, it is my sincere opinion that the Constitution ought to be revised, and that the first Congress meeting under it, ought to prepare and recommend to the States for ratification, the most satisfactory provisions for all essential rights, particularly the rights of Conscience in the fullest latitude, the freedom of the press, trials by jury, security against general warrants etc."[19]

As his later correspondence indicates, the sentiments espoused in the Eve letter became the campaign slogan he adopted. "It is my wish, particularly, to see specific provision made on the subject of the *Rights of Conscience, the Freedom of the Press, Trials by Jury, Exemption from General Warrants*" (January 27, 1789). On February 2, 1789, Madison was elected by a comfortable margin over his opponent, James Monroe. Ralph Ketcham called it "a remarkable personal tribute to Madison in a district 'rigged' against him."

On March 15, 1789, Jefferson wrote from Paris a highly significant response to Madison's letter of the previous October. "In the arguments in favor of a declaration of rights, you omit one which has great weight with me, the legal check which it puts into the hands of the judiciary. This is a body, which if rendered independent, & kept strictly to their own department merits great confidence for their learning and integrity."[20] This argument was quite convincing to Madison and was used, as we will soon see, in his presentation to the first Congress. It may be construed as ironic that it would be in the administration of Jefferson, 1803, when Madison was secretary of state, that John Marshall wrote the Supreme Court decision in *Marbury* v. *Madison* that established judicial review as a principle upon which the nation now firmly rests.

New York: Amendments and Honor, 1789

Perhaps influenced by the heady atmosphere at Montpelier, Madison's home, on Constitution Day in 1990, James MacGregor Burns, after speaking of the sage of Orange County as truly the "father of the Bill of Rights," argued that the remarkable thing about the political climate two centuries ago was trust. He rightly noted that enough delegates to the 1788 Virginia Convention, like those at similar gatherings in the other states, set aside their reservations about the Philadelphia document and voted for it just because they trusted the promises of those who gave assurances that the first order of business for the new nation should be consideration of amendments.

On July 21, 1789, Congressman Madison addressed his colleagues. He "begged the House to indulge him in the further consideration of amendments to the Constitution." Encountering stiff opposition, Madison returned to the issue on August 13.

> He would remind gentlemen that there were many who conceived amendments of some kind necessary and proper in themselves; while others who are not so well satisfied of the necessity and propriety, may think they are rendered expedient from some other consideration. Is it desirable to keep up a division among the people of the United States on a point in which they consider their most essential rights are concerned? If this is an object worthy the attention of such a numerous part of our constituents, why should we decline taking it into our consideration, and thereby promote that spirit of urbanity and unanimity which the Government itself stands in need of for its more full support?
>
> Already has the subject been delayed much longer than could have been wished. If after having fixed a day for taking it into consideration, we should put it off again, a spirit of jealousy may be excited, and not allayed without great inconvenience.[21]

Madison encountered dissent from those members who felt more important matters required attention. Representative Lawrence stated, "Certainly the people in general are more anxious to see the Government in operation, than speculative amendments upon an untried constitution."

In his sharpest rejoinder Madison appealed to the honor of the body.

> I admit, with the worthy gentleman who preceded me, that a great number of the community are solicitous to see the Gov-

ernment carried into operation; but I believe that there is a considerable part also anxious to secure those rights which they are apprehensive are endangered by the present constitution. Now, considering the full confidence they reposed at the time of its adoption in their future representatives, I think we ought to pursue the subject to effect. I confess it has already appeared to me, in point of candor and good faith, as well as policy, to be incumbent on the first Legislature of the United States, at their first session, to make such alterations in the constitution as will give satisfaction, without injuring or destroying any of its vital principles.[22]

The difficulty Madison encountered in convincing his colleagues to consider rights amendments suggests that Professor Burns's observations about "trust" may not be universally applicable to the founders.

The debates over the amendments are detailed and have been analyzed by numerous scholars. In all this examination it is clear that Madison's congressional leadership was the primary impetus for what came to be the Bill of Rights. Prodded by Madison, aware of citizen concerns, the lawmakers ultimately turned to the task of keeping a promise.

In the initial stages the amendments were to be incorporated into the text at appropriate points. Rep. Roger Sherman vigorously opposed this procedure from the outset. But it was not until August 19 that Sherman prevailed in his motion to separate the amendments from the original Constitution. Madison had considered it a question more of form than substance. It is arguable that the form became substance when the amendments advanced from mere insertions in a complex document, to the entity that is the "Bill of Rights."

Originally, what we know as the First Amendment was the

third of twelve offered to the states for ratification. Rejection of one and two made "free exercise" our first liberty. Frequently the two religion clauses are considered in isolation from the remaining parts of the First Amendment. While this procedure has advantages, it may appear on occasion that priority is being assigned on the basis of position. Such assumptions are incorrect and miss the value of viewing the amendment as a whole. This caveat having been stated, it is desirable for purposes of this study to extract, as much as possible, from the debates in Congress relative to religion-state matters.

The first sixteen words of the third amendment submitted to the states read, "Congress shall make no law respecting an establishment of religion, or prohibiting the free exercise thereof." The impetus for their inclusion was commitment to freedom of conscience as a principle. But while that conviction was without reservation on the part of men like Jefferson and Madison, it was not a universal sentiment for those who gathered in New York in 1789. Some of the states, notably Massachusetts, still had restrictive language in their laws that provided toleration at best, and that only to Protestants. Several states had established religions. So the courageous stand for a free conscience at the federal level was frequently a means of self-protection. If there could be no national religion consistent with a particular state tradition, then clearly it was in the interest of the states to assure federal protection of variant religious traditions.

On August 15 Madison engaged his colleagues in an extended discussion of wording on the religion amendment. That discussion has recently been the subject of Chief Justice William Rehnquist's unique interpretation. Responding to concerns over the draft as it then read, "no religion shall be established by law," Madison suggested adding national before the word religion. The problem lies in the fact that there is no clarity as to the objections by

Rep. Huntington of Rhode Island that prompted Madison's response. Rehnquist jumped to the conclusion that by using "national" Madison intended to allow nonpreferential treatment of all religions. He feels this proves that Madison did not "conform to the 'wall of separation' between church and state which latter day commentators have ascribed to him." Two things need to be noted. First, the word "national" was never defined by Madison and was in any event almost immediately dropped by him after a single objection. Second, Madison had an expansive intention when he used the term "national" in other contexts. "Religious proclamations by the Executive recommending thanksgiving and feasts . . . seem to imply and certainly nourish the erroneous idea of a *national* religion." And, as we have noted earlier, Madison's opposition to the General Assessment Bill in 1784–85 clearly placed him in opposition to plural establishments of any kind.[23]

On August 24 the House sent seventeen amendments to the Senate. The third read, "Congress shall make no law establishing religion, or prohibiting the free exercise thereof; nor shall the rights of conscience be infringed." A Senate motion was made to strike "religion, or prohibiting the free exercise thereof" and to substitute "one religious sect or society in preference to others." That was eighteenth-century nonpreferentialism. It was, as Madison knew, the most insidious form of establishment. The motion was defeated in the Senate. Another amendment, "Congress shall make no law establishing any particular denomination of religion in preference to another . . ." was also rejected. As finally reported the Senate accepted the House wording but struck the clause concerning "rights of conscience."

In a Senate/House conference committee there was a lingering effort to have reference to establishing a single sect. The committee rejected that approach. Finally on September 24 the House sent a message to the Senate indicating it would agree with other

Senate amendments provided the amendment on religion read, "Congress shall make no law respecting an establishment of religion, or prohibiting the free exercise thereof." The Senate agreed on September 25.

Madison had prevailed in spite of the fact that probably the majority of the members of Congress saw no problem with establishment of religion in principle. And there were many who would have blanched at the thought of granting freedom of conscience to non-Christians. Madison so noted in his October 17, 1789, letter to Jefferson. "I am sure that the rights of Conscience in particular, if submitted to public definition would be narrowed much more than they are likely ever to be by an assumed power." Supporting this view was the fate of an additional article proposed by Madison, which read, "No State shall infringe the equal rights of conscience, nor the freedom of speech, or of the press, nor of the right to trial by jury in criminal cases." Addressing his peers in the House on August 17 Madison said he considered his proposed amendment "the most valuable amendment on the whole list." The Senate demurred. Victory on that front would have to wait until 1868 and the Fourteenth Amendment. On September 25 Congress sent the amendments to the states.

Notes

1. "Madison letter to Thomas Jefferson, Oct. 24, 1787," in G. Hunt, *The Writings of James Madision,* vol. 10 (New York: G. P. Putnam's Sons, 1910), p. 217.
2. Ibid.
3. Ibid., p. 244.
4. Ibid., p. 234.
5. Ibid., vol. 17, p. 527.

6. Ibid., vol. 10, p. 526.

7. Ibid.

8. Ibid., p. 541.

9. Reuben E. Alley, *A History of Baptists in Virginia* (Richmond: Virginia Baptist General Board, 1973), p. 116.

10. G. Hunt, *The Writings of James Madison*, vol. 11, p. 5.

11. Ibid., vol. 10, p. 542.

12. Ralph Ketcham, *James Madison* (New York: Macmillan, 1971), p. 251. Ketcham goes so far as to describe this undocumented meeting as "cordial." One example of the growth of this myth, which seems to have a life of its own, was the testimony of Jimmy Allen, director of the Southern Baptist Radio and Television Commission. An intelligent, reasonable man, Allen said of the First Amendment, when he testified before the Senate Judiciary Committee in 1982, "The fact is that James Madison was the author of that first amendment. He did it out of a deal he made basically at Madison Leland Park in Virginia where a Baptist preacher, John Leland, struck the deal because he was considering running against Madison for the Constitutional Assembly because of his concern for the persecution we felt and the necessity to guard religious liberty by some separation of the role of the state and the role of the church" (U.S. Congress, Senate Judiciary Committee Hearings, *Proposed Constitutional Amendment to Permit Voluntary Prayer*, 1982, p. 161).

13. Hunt, *Writings of James Madison*, vol. 17, p. 526.

14. Irving Brant, *James Madison: Commander in Chief* (New York: The Bobbs-Merril Co., 1961), vol. 2, p. 216.

15. Bernard Schwartz, *The Bill of Rights* (New York: Chelsea House, 1971), vol. 2, p. 830.

16. Hunt, *Writings of James Madison*, vol. 11, p. 28.

17. Ibid., p. 213.

18. Ibid., p. 297.

19. Ibid., p. 405.

20. Ibid., vol. 12, p. 13.

21. Schwartz, *The Bill of Rights*, vol. 2, p. 1062.

22. Ibid., p. 1065.

23. Leonard Levy in his book *The Establishment Clause* (New York: Macmillan, 1986), p. 84, makes the following summary in reference to the question of plural establishments.

The history of the drafting of the establishment clause does not provide us with an understanding of what was meant by "an establishment of religion." To argue, however, as proponents of a narrow interpretation do, that the amendment permits congressional aid and support to religion in general or to all denominations without discrimination, leads to the impossible conclusion that the First Amendment added to Congress's power. Nothing supports such a conclusion. Every bit of evidence goes to prove that the First Amendment, like the others, was intended to restrict Congress to its enumerated powers. Because Congress possessed no power under the Constitution to legislate on matters concerning religion, Congress has no such power even in the absence of the First Amendment. It is therefore unreasonable, even fatuous, to believe that an express prohibition of power—"Congress shall make no law respecting an establishment of religion"—vests or creates the power, previously nonexistent, of supporting religion by aid to all religious groups. The Bill of Rights, as Madison said, was not framed, "to imply powers not meant to be included in the enumeration."

3

The Nineteenth Century

The Court Record

From 1792, when the Bill of Rights was officially included as part of the Constitution, until 1940 few cases related to the religion clauses of the First Amendment came before the Supreme Court. A significant and determinative decision was reached in *Barron v. Baltimore*, 1833, when Chief Justice Marshall wrote concerning the Bill of Rights, "These amendments contain no expression indicating an intention to apply them to the State governments. This Court cannot so apply them."

There was little argument that could be advanced to counter Marshall on this assertion since Madison had specifically called for such an application in his version of what would become the First Amendment and that language was rejected by the Senate.

In 1815 an act of the Virginia legislature was challenged in the Court. That act of 1801 rescinded a 1776 action by the Virginia legislators that had confirmed the right of the Episcopal Church to possess all the lands and property previously held by the

Anglican Church. Deciding the case on the principle that "the division of an empire creates no forfeiture of previously-vested rights of property," the Court, in *Terrett* v. *Taylor*, asserted that it was consonant with "the common sense of mankind and the maxims of eternal justice." The decision was not based upon any specific constitutional provision and was heard by the Court because it related to prerevolutionary actions of the Virginia assembly.

In 1844 the Court upheld the validity of a will establishing a college for orphans in Pennsylvania although that will "required no ecclesiastical, missionary, or minister of any sect whatsoever, shall ever hold or exercise any station or duty whatever in the said college." Although the case dealt with other issues as well relating to the will, the key point was made by Justice Joseph Story in *Vidal* v. *Girard's Executors* when he wrote, "We are satisfied that there is nothing in the devise establishing the college, or in the regulations and restrictions contained therein, which are inconsistent with the Christian religion, or are opposed to any known policy of the State of Pennsylvania." In his challenge to Girard's will Daniel Webster said to the Court, "No fault can be found with Girard for wishing a marble college to bear his name forever, but it is not valuable unless it has a fragrance of Christianity about it." In 1948, commenting on that decision, Justice Felix Frankfurter noted, "In sustaining Stephen Girard's will, this Court referred to the inevitable conflicts engendered by matters 'connected with religious polity' and particularly 'in a country composed of such a variety of religious sects as our country.' "[1] Again, the First Amendment was not a part of the decision.

After the Civil War the Walnut Street (Presbyterian) Church of Louisville was fractured over the question of slavery and members were divided over whether future allegiance should be with the Presbyterian General Assembly of the United States or the Presbyterian Church of the Confederate States. Because some members involved lived in Indiana, the Court accepted jurisdiction. Again, with no reference to the First Amendment, the Court ruled on quite clear grounds. "Religious organizations come before us in the same attitude as other voluntary associations for benevolent or charitable purposes, and their rights of property, or of contract, are equally under the protection of the law, and the actions of their members subject to its restraints." Continuing, Justice Samuel Freeman Miller noted, "The rights of such bodies to use of the property must be determined by the ordinary principles which govern voluntary associations. . . . This ruling admits of no inquiry into the existing religious opinions of those who comprise the legal or regular organization" (*Watson* v. *Jones* 13 Wallace 679 [1872]).

Up to that point the Court's rare opinions on the subject of religion had been unrelated to First Amendment issues. In *Reynolds* v. *United States* in 1879 the Court dealt with a matter of free exercise related to Mormons, but only because the issue involved not a state but a territory governed by Congress. Two similar cases followed.[2]

In 1892 Justice David Brewer wrote for the Court in an immigration dispute that "this is a Christian nation."[3] In 1899 the Court ruled that establishing a hospital in the District of Columbia that was run by a sisterhood of the Roman Catholic Church was not an establishment because the hospital is "purely a secular one."[4]

Of all the nineteenth-century cases the Brewer decision of 1892 creates the gravest concern. There was a troubling undercurrent in the Court's language that presaged the current debate of 1993. Ruling that a church could employ a minister from another nation without running afoul of a congressional restriction on hiring aliens,[5] Brewer wrote in *Church of the Holy Trinity* v.

the United States that the United States is a "religious nation," and went on at length to describe its religion as Christianity.

> In *Updegraph* v. *Com.*, it was decided that, "Christianity, general Christianity, is, and always has been, a part of the common law of Pennsylvania; . . . not Christianity with an established church, and tithes, and spiritual courts; but Christianity with liberty of conscience to all men." And in *People* v. *Ruggles,* Chancellor Kent, the great commentator on American law, speaking as Chief Justice of the Supreme Court of New York, said: "The people of this State, in common with the people of this country, profess the general doctrines of Christianity, as the rule of their faith and practice; and to scandalize the author of these doctrines is not only, in a religious point of view, extremely impious, but even in respect to the obligations due to society, is a gross violation of decency and good order. . . . The free, equal, and undisturbed enjoyment of religious opinion, whatever it may be, and free and decent discussions on any religious subject, is granted and secured; but to revile, with malicious and blasphemous contempt, the religion professed by almost the whole community, is an abuse of that right. Nor are we bound, by any expressions in the Constitution, as some have strangely supposed, either not to punish at all, or to punish indiscriminately, the like attacks upon the religion of Mahomet or of the Grand Lama; and for this plain reason, that the case assumes that we are a Christian people, and the morality of the country is deeply ingrafted upon Christianity, and not upon the doctrines or worship of those impostors."[6]

Madison on the Notion of a Christian America

The arrival in the United States, between 1820 and 1860, of large numbers of Catholic immigrants and a sizable number of German

Jews set the stage for changing church and state relationship. Professor John Wilson of Princeton University has written:

> After the Civil War the ethnic multiplication and religious diversification that had begun in the previous era could no longer remain unrecognized and unacknowledged. As might be expected, public schools became a battleground (even before the Civil War) over the interrelationship of temporal and spiritual authority structures. . . . It is interesting that where the "burden of religious pluralism" was explicitly recognized, a position favoring a neutral relationship between church and state emerged that clearly repudiated the assumptions underlying "republican protestantism."[7]

E. Digby Baltzell made comparable points in his sociological study, *The Protestant Establishment.*

Wilson observed that both Catholic and Protestant systems of thought were rattled by this changing scene. While Catholics were adjusting to relationships that clashed with European models in their new American Catholicism, Protestants were shaken by a challenge to their belief in a national messianism that saw Roman Catholics as enemies of the faith. For vast numbers of Protestants the views expressed in eighteenth-century sermons by Presbyterian divine Samuel Davies remained normative well into the twentieth. "The greatest part of Europe is corrupted with the idolatry, superstition, and debaucheries of the church of Rome, and groans under its tyranny."[8]

Davies felt that natural disasters, such as earthquakes, were used by God to punish Catholics, such as in Lisbon in 1755. But for Davies sin was not confined to Roman Catholicism. Protestantism was also corrupt; he asserted that Protestant countries, where true religion was to be found, if anywhere, had abandoned the truth. Therefore God could well be employing the signs of the times to warn that he would use the power of popery and France to chastise Britain. As the modern observer of religious evangelism in the United States examines the preaching of Billy Graham or Pat Robertson there is an eerie similarity with Davies' proclamations.[9] He asserted that "Popish tyranny" would last, according to Revelation 12:6, for 1,260 years but he was confounded because he didn't know when that period commenced. The French and Indian War might be the "commencement of this grand decisive conflict between the Lamb and the beast," but Davies could not be certain. Therefore, God might be using the Pope to punish the recalcitrant British Protestants.

In 1833, less than three years before his death James Madison confronted the growing number of public pronouncements that identified Christianity with the nation. He chose to respond to a letter addressed to him from Jasper Adams, president of the College of Charleston in South Carolina. In a printed sermon delivered to a convention in Charleston, Adams argued against the view that Christianity "had no connection with our civil constitutions of government." Rather, he insisted, "the people of the United States have retained the Christian religion as the foundation of their civil, legal, and political institutions." In order to strengthen his position he sent the sermon to many prominent men of his day. In addition to Madison, he received replies from two justices of the Supreme Court who together served a total of sixty-nine years on the bench.

John Marshall wrote, "The American population is entirely Christian, and with us, Christianity and religion are identified." Joseph Story was more expansive. "I have read it with uncommon satisfaction. I think its tone and spirit excellent. My own private judgment has long been (and every day's experience more and more confirms me in it) that government can not long exist without an alliance with religion; and that Christianity is indispensable to the true interests and solid foundations of free government."

One may easily relate those sentiments affirming a "de facto" establishment mentality in the mid-nineteenth century to a new variety of the same thinking being espoused under the guise of "nonpreferentialism." Some members of the current Supreme Court, with encouragement from the religious right, have begun a campaign to detract from the phrase "separation of church and state" in order to promulgate an alternative theory. Chief Justice Rehnquist wrote in his dissent in the *Jaffree* case that, "The 'wall of separation between church and state' is a metaphor based on bad history, a metaphor which has proved useless as a guide to judging. It should be frankly and explicitly abandoned."

In fact the metaphor is "history."It comes directly from Jefferson's 1802 letter to the Danbury (Connecticut) Baptist Association. The history is clear. Jefferson interpreted the First Amendment's religion clauses as "building" that wall. Since we have demonstrated that Jefferson was the force who ultimately convinced Madison to favor a bill of rights and, further, that the correspondence between them makes it clear that on the subject of free exercise they were of one mind and, finally, that Madison used a similar metaphor when he wrote of "the line of separation between the rights of religion and the Civil authority," it is the height of arrogance to dismiss the metaphor as "based on bad history." It would be far more rational for Chief Justice Rehnquist to assert that he finds flaws in the principles espoused by Jefferson. After all, Jefferson was not drawing his metaphor from books or second-hand recollections of events in 1789, he was setting forth a principle he was convinced underlay the words of the amendment based on his lengthy correspondence with Madison. There is absolutely no evidence that either Madison or any other member from that first Congress challenged the president's understanding of the meaning. If we might, then, approach the subject as Madison did on the floor of the House in 1789, we could be about the business of exchanging ideas on the First Amendment legacy.

Madison likely did not have access to the remarks by Marshall and Story when he responded to Jasper Adams, but his reply to Adams' sermon can rightly be appropriated as a response to both justices.

> Until Holland ventured on the experiment of combining a liberal toleration with the establishment of a particular creed, it was taken for granted, that an exclusive & intolerant establishment was essential, and notwithstanding the light thrown on the subject by that experiment, the prevailing opinion in Europe, England not excepted, has been that Religion could not be preserved without the support of Govt. nor Govt. be supported witht. an established religion, that there must be at least an alliance of some sort between them.
>
> It remained for North America to bring the great & interesting subject to a fair, and finally to a decisive test.
>
> In the Colonial State of the Country, there were four examples, R. I. N. J. Penna. and Delaware, and the greater part of N. Y. where there were no religious Establishments; the support of Religion being left to the voluntary associations & contributions of individuals; and certainly the religious condition of those Colonies, will well bear a comparison with that where establishment existed.[10]

Madison saw this decisive test as having been administered in the growing number of states with no establishment. In the same year he wrote his letter to Adams, Massachusetts finally became the last state to disestablish the church. Madison used the fifty years of state experiences to make his case. He was secure in his conviction that it had been proved that religion "does not need the support of Govt. and it will scarcely be contended that Government has suffered by the exemption of Religion from its cognizance, or its pecuniary aid." Here he was speaking of the Virginia experience that dated from 1785. Interestingly, he used the same term employed in the first remonstrance that same year—"Religion is wholly exempt from its cognizance."

Madison then turned to the consistency of the policy he advocated and admitted freely that there were problems.

> I must admit moreover that it may not be easy, in every possible case, to trace the line of separation between the rights of religion and the Civil authority with such distinctness as to avoid collisions & doubts on unessential points. The tendency to a usurpation on one side or the other, or to a corrupting coalition or alliance between them, will be best guarded agst. by an entire abstinence of the Govt. from interference in any way whatever, beyond the necessity of preserving public order, & protecting each sect agst. trespasses on its legal rights by others.[11]

So Madison concluded his final remarks on the subject of separation of church and state by using a variation on the term and by exploring the difficult areas of conflict. Here he moved from history to prognosis, fully aware that the public mood was likely as negative toward his views as his hand and fingers were "averse to the pen as they are awkward in the use of it." Reason convinced the last of the founders that public order and religious freedom will be protected and guarded by "separation between the rights of religion and the Civil authority."

This is the case to be made in 1993, not an empty debate over original intent and contradictions. To note that Madison voted for employment of a chaplain in the House of Representatives in 1789 begs the question whether, based upon the thoughtful analysis of a lifelong commitment to free exercise and disestablishment, such a vote means anything at all. Perhaps, in a nation with a predominantly Christian population and with a Congress almost totally of that persuasion, Mr. Madison felt confrontation on this point was a collision on an unessential issue. We do not know, but in a multicultural mix that has expanded Protestants from a dozen denominations to hundreds, has seen an explosion in Catholic population since 1850, the development of the largest Jewish population in the world, the emancipation of a slave population with a religion distinctly a part of the black heritage, a growing concern for Native American practices, a state with tens of thousands of Buddhist citizens, a large and vocal Islamic community, a growing variety of sects and groups that defy definition in old categories, and the effective voices of agnostics and atheists, in such a mix Madison just might have seen the chaplaincy as indeed a collision over an essential point. We don't know, and we must pose the question for ourselves, not for our distinguished forebear.

To hold doggedly to the precise application of free exercise of religion in the earliest days of the Republic as recited even by the likes of John Marshall is, in Jefferson's words, to "narrow its operation." The principle operating with both Jefferson and Madison was one of inclusiveness, not exclusiveness. While their vision stopped short of insisting upon equality for women, blacks, and Native Americans, their principles espoused in the nation's documents moved toward greater and greater inclusiveness.

It is altogether probable that Madison was out of step with the sentiments of mid-nineteenth-century America. Dumas Malone doubted that either he or Jefferson could have been elected to the presidency by that time. The reason for that observation was their outspoken Christian humanism without orthodoxy. But if their thoughts failed to sway their fellow citizens in the eighteen hundreds, their principles offer the most rational point of beginning for addressing a multicultural nation entering the twenty-first century.

Notes

1. See *McCollum v. Board of Education*, 333 U.S. 203 (1948). Cited from Justice Felix Frankfurter's opinion for the Court.

2. *Davis v. Beason*, 133 US 333 (1890), *The Late Corporation of the Church of Jesus Christ of Latter-Day Saints v. United States*, 136 US 1 (1890).

3. *Church of the Holy Trinity v. United States* (1892). See Joseph Tussman, *The Supreme Court on Church and State* (Oxford University Press, 1962), pp. 40-41.

4. *Bradfield v. Roberts*, 175 US 291 (1899).

5. *Church of the Holy Trinity v. United States*, 143 US 226 (1892).

6. Ibid., p. 107.

7. John Wilson, "Church and State in America," in *James Madison on Religious Liberty*, ed. Robert S. Alley (Buffalo, N.Y.: Prometheus Books, 1985), p. 105.

8. Samuel Davies, *Sermons on Important Subjects* (Philadelphia: Presbyterian Board of Publication, 1864), vol. 3, pp. 209-210.

9. One recalls Billy Graham asserting that God was using Communist Russia, later China, to punish a failed Christian America. Or again, reflect on Pat Robertson asserting in 1981 that the United States is mentioned only once in the Bible (in Ezekiel).

10. "Letter from Madison to Jasper Adams, Spring 1833," in *James Madison on Religious Liberty*, ed. Robert S. Alley (Buffalo, N.Y.: Prometheus Books, 1985), pp. 87-88.

11. "A Bill for Establishing Religious Freedom in Virginia," written by Thomas Jefferson and adopted, with minor revision, by the Virginia General Assembly in 1785.

4

Presidential Leadership: Divine Mandate?

Since the Supreme Court, in 1833, had properly assessed the words of the First Amendment to exclude jurisdiction over state legislation and the Congress seldom ventured into the arena of church and state, the presidential "bully pulpit" was the only national forum that occasionally addressed religion and state matters. Presidential proclamations concerning prayer were primary sources of executive action on that front. Lincoln infrequently made reference to God and President Grant on one occasion affirmed his belief in separation of church and state. It seems wise to pause to examine, in brief compass, some characteristics of the presidents that interacted with what most historians consider a century of de facto Protestant establishment. Indeed, from a presidential perspective that sentiment has dominated in the White House, long after its disappearance in the nation at large, even through the Bush years, with the exception of presidents FDR, JFK, and Jimmy Carter.

Categorizing historical figures is a risky endeavor. That established, it seems possible to identify at least three types of presidents who have served the United States since 1789. For that purpose the language of the 1960s concerning ethics provides a convenient frame of reference. That era spawned the term "new morality" and set off a controversy in every theological school in the country. In simple terms there were three alternatives generally employed. First, there were goal-oriented persons; second, those who relied upon past history and law; and third, those representing the new wave of situation ethics based on a pragmatic response under the rubric of love. Slippery definitions of love made the third category difficult to identify. If we examine the men who have served as president, it is possible to apply this three-part scheme as a useful descriptive device to most of them.

Goal-oriented individuals are presumed to function from basic principles that focus on the future. Crass simplification may reduce this to the end justifying the means. But if we apply this definition in an even-handed way to presidents of the past, we can identify men who envisioned a more perfect union grounded in constitutional principles. For them future generations would be a more accurate barometer of their performance. Such perception was evident in Madison's last letter to Jefferson, previously cited. Madison affirmed, "We cannot be deprived of the happy consciousness of the pure devotion to the public good with which we discharged the trusts committed to us. And I indulge a confidence that sufficient evidence will find its way to another generation, to ensure, after we are gone, whatever of justice may be withheld whilst we are here."[1]

There are at least two roots for those who fit this mold. One is the commitment to democratic resolutions of conflict within the context of natural rights. The other is a religious background that diminishes authoritarian models, found most frequently among congregational Protestantism and Unitarianism. From those individuals in this category one may expect statements of fundamental principles cast in terms of justice and freedom. In the nineteenth century Madison, Jefferson, and Lincoln come to mind. In the present century there has been little to encourage the continuation of that stream other than President Carter. Adlai Stevenson fits the model but failed to attain the office. It is too early to assess President Clinton, but he may fit this model.

A second type of president is evident in the lives of Franklin Roosevelt and John Kennedy. They, along with a few others, imbibed of an episcopal model of church governance that was tempered by pragmatism. This *via media* plotted a middle course that offered sufficient doctrinal breadth and fluidity to produce a principled, realistic pragmatism in politics. Presidents in this category were seldom self-conscious about their religion. In the case of Kennedy, he exemplified post–Vatican II thinking in his religious assertions. Episcopal Bishop Pike probably understood this tradition when he described the American political scene as "the middle way."[2] This tradition seems to fit the category of situation ethics. At least in the political arena there is strong support for the notion of a pragmatism that uses "God talk" while keeping a sharp eye for the changing character of the American population. These men are usually able to deal with the realities of social and cultural change with a greater degree of flexibility than their colleagues of the third tradition.

By far the greatest number of presidents have emerged from a Calvinist Protestant tradition heavily indoctrinated with authoritarian legalisms. Grounded in past laws and doctrines even liberal-spirited persons like Woodrow Wilson ultimately remained captive to a rigid orthodox Calvinism. God's laws were immutable. True enough, Jefferson spoke of natural law, but it was always grounded for him in reason functioning in the present. In contrast, Calvinism looks back to a golden era of revelation that must forever dominate reason and practice. Ronald Reagan, captured by a fundamentalism of the political right, was an easy mark for extremely illiberal expressions on social issues. George Bush, in contrast, was nonideological and pragmatic, but these two traits led him to a presumably practical coalition with ideologues with whom he had no fundamental sympathy. The result was catastrophic, a pragmatic ideologue possessing no ideology. No wonder Bush's 1992 campaign was confused.

For this third group it was frequently true that religion and politics were in tension awaiting the taming of the latter by the former. The extreme of this sentiment may be found in President William McKinley's comment on the conquest of the Philippines: "There was nothing left for us to do but to take them all, and to educate the Filipinos, and uplift and civilize and Christianize them, and by God's grace do the very best we could by them as our fellowmen for whom Christ also dies."[3] In its most severe forms this perspective has hatched American Messianism.

Protestant "Establishment" in a New Century

In the years from 1860 to 1920 the power and hegemony of the Protestant majority was under enormous stress. What had been a presumed Protestant establishment in the United States was exposed to serious challenge and erosion by the influx of immigrants after the Civil War. Professor John Wilson feels that "the most fascinating development (from 1820 to 1860) was the attempt by the evangelical forces in the United States to recover in an informal way what had been their legal position before disestablishment. During this 'era of republican Protestantism' interdenominational agencies developed a great 'united front' that aspired to make the U.S. a Protestant Christian republic, in substance if not in form."[4]

That notion of the Christian state had not disappeared by 1920. True, as Wilson states, Americans began to discuss, as Protestants, Catholics, and Jews, religious pluralism. And certainly he is correct that "the existence of two authority structures seems to have been recognized in principle if not always honored in practice, and the historical alternatives of subordinating one to the other were not widely viewed as plausible formal options." Wilson concludes that the current debate is between those who see encouragement of religion as intrinsic to our culture and those who believe government should not give any aid or assistance to religion. "In short, this is a battle between believers in benevolent neutrality and proponents of strict separation."[5]

As we move closer to our own time Wilson's dual model has been changed with the addition of a third alternative. Since 1962 a growing, vocal Christian contingent, later to be embraced by presidents Reagan and Bush in the eighties, rejected not only "strict separation" but "benevolent neutrality" as well. In reality, there has never been a time when the voices of the heirs to Puritan theocracy have been quiet. But what Wilson saw as a reasoned battle between two views of church/state relations, is today a fundamentalist-defined conflict between true believers and infidels. For thirty years that infidel has been personified as the Supreme Court. Fellow travelers have been the American Civil Liberties Union, humanists, and Jews.

The Theological Problem

By nature a democracy is restricted from enforcing authoritarianism and ideological conformity. Even divested of the Bill of Rights, this is the clear message of the Constitution. The Christian faith is, by definition, authoritarian and doctrinally driven. To be sure,

Christians have spilt buckets of blood over whose authority and doctrine. The Davies sermonizing of 1755 is one minor example. From the moment that some ecclesiastical figure read the Gospel of Matthew and arrogated to himself spiritual power and authority in the name of Christ, the Christian church has promulgated human interpretations of a man's life as binding upon all humanity. Different voices were heard and silenced in the name of that authority. The exclusivism of Christianity became its fundamental principle, its driving force. A great and powerful institution emerged from the rubble of the Roman Empire to dominate Europe in the Middle Ages. The human spirit continually challenged the hegemony of this ecclesiastical hierarchy. That challenge bore fruit in alternative institutions in the sixteenth-century Reformation, institutions that almost instantly presumed the same exclusivism, authority, and power claimed by the Vatican. In principle there is no essential difference between the two traditions. Both believe they possess the only truth about reality, that those who fail to believe are doomed to eternal punishment, and that their exclusive God acts in history. It is this last assertion that becomes the major difficulty for the modern nation state. For by insisting that nations are functionaries of deity, a single deity known only to Christians, democracy becomes an anomalous entity.

Even for many Christian citizens who have come to terms with the diversity of a democratic state, there is a lingering dogma of exclusivism that lies dormant. Protestants and Catholics alike tend to view the historical process as in some way controlled by the deity. Thus the nation becomes in some respect the handmaid of God.

The idea of a divine mandate for America, and thus the presidency, took on new meaning when the United States entered upon the stage of world history in 1917. By 1919 this nation was a dominant world player and it was on that stage that American messianism blossomed in the actions of President Wilson.

President Woodrow Wilson

Commenting upon America's involvement in World War I President Woodrow Wilson said: "For liberty is a spiritual conception, and when men take up arms to set other men free, there is something sacred and holy in the warfare." This sentiment rings true to an American tradition. Yet, it is only a few steps further to turn democracy into a clarion call to crusade when the principles so well phrased by Wilson become little more than slogans. It seems that the line between those principles and a nativistic Americanism may have been crossed in 1917. Louis Hartz, testifying before the Senate Foreign Relations Committee in 1968, suggested precisely that.

> The matter of the nationalist response goes back, in fact, to the moment of the migration itself. For when the English Puritan comes to America, he is no longer completely "English," which means that he has to find a new national identity. And where is that identity to come from if not from Puritanism itself, the ideal part of which he has extracted from the English whole and which alone he possesses. Hence the part becomes, as it were, a new whole and Puritanism itself blossoms into "Americanism."[6]

The term "Americanism" did not actually appear in our vocabulary until the twentieth century, when "collectivists replaced aristocrats as the symbol of alien ideology."[7] Hartz believed that a new kind of American "Messianism" began with Woodrow

Wilson, coincident with Vladimir Lenin's rise to power. This created a "tug of war between two attitudes . . . one, the Wilsonian attitude of seeking to impose our institutions, seeking to evangelize the results of a peculiar experience, and another which seeks to recognize the relativity of historical situations and to work within that relativity."

Wilson's addresses support the Hartz thesis. In his war message to Congress on April 2, 1917, Wilson affirmed:

> The world must be made safe for democracy; its peace must be planted upon tested foundations of political liberty. . . . We desire no conquest, no dominion. . . . We are but one of the champions of the rights of mankind. We shall be satisfied when those rights have been made as secure as the faith and the freedom of the nations can make them. . . . To such a task we can dedicate our lives and our fortunes, everything that we are and everything that we have, with the pride of those who know that the day has come when America is privileged to spend her blood and her might for the principles that gave her birth and happiness and the peace which she has treasured. God helping her, she can do no other.[8]

God is mentioned only once, at the last, and there in the paraphrase of Martin Luther facing attacks upon his writings by a hostile church. There is no gainsaying the fact that national turmoil and crisis call for leadership that can inspire and encourage. Wilson gave both in a speech measured in tone, literate in structure. But like many such messages, it is cast in such stark terms of good and evil that later failures and blindnesses tend to discount it. The problem for any democracy is clearly illustrated in the Wilson dilemma. How do you enforce freedom without risking it? How does one enforce peace without losing it?

Wilson's optimism for the future was unbounded that day in April. He spoke of Russia as a "fit partner." Referring to events in that country in the "last few weeks," he said, "Russia was known by those who knew it best to have been always in fact democratic at heart, in all the vital habits of her thought, in all the intimate relationships of her people that spoke their natural instinct, their habitual attitude towards life." Then Wilson reached into the future once again, making a further observation:

> The autocracy that crowned the summit of her political struc-
> ture, long as it had stood and terrible as was the reality of
> its power, was not in fact Russian in origin, character, or
> purpose, and now it has been shaken off and the great gen-
> erous Russian people have been added in all their native majesty
> and might to the forces that are fighting for freedom in the
> world, for justice and for peace. Here is a fit partner for a League
> of Honor.[9]

Of course Wilson's Russian dream turned sour and a seventy-five-year conflict ensued, with the United States leadership personifying the Soviets as enemies of God. Presidents Wilson and Bush seemed to bookend an incredible era of promise and disaster.

The United States had emerged as a world leader at precisely the same moment as Lenin began his construction of the Soviet Union. Reaction to a foreign war brought our nation to that pinnacle in 1917. Later reactions to Hitler, Stalin, Mao, and Ho Chi Minh brought forth exercise of power that established American leadership in a dangerous world. As foes crumbled or weakened the United States reacted to Grenada, Panama, and Iraq in order to sustain its prestige in the world. Always the cry was the same—make the world safe for democracy. We even had the audacity to apply this notion to Kuwait. Magnificent struggles in the name of messianism became less grand, falling into total disrepute in 1991 in the sound-bite, computer-chip war against Iraq.

Now at the very moment when the policies of the past seventy-five years may be tested with resolve rather than revolvers, we face an economic crisis born of greed and corruption that threatens to allow eastern Europe to sink back into the disastrous warfare of previous centuries.

Messianism was never quite consistent with democratic principles. In a world threatened by peace it becomes an absurdity. That messianism, espoused by many presidents, found deep roots in a religious mentality honed upon an exclusive claim to knowledge of deity.

In November, 1918, President Wilson observed:

God has in His good pleasure given us peace. It has not come as a mere cessation of arms, a mere relief from the strain and tragedy of war. It has come as a great triumph of right. Complete victory has brought us, not peace alone, but the confident promise of a new day as well in which justice shall replace force and jealous intrigue among the nations. Our gallant armies have participated in a triumph which is not marred or stained by any purpose of selfish aggression. In a righteous cause they have won immortal glory and have nobly served their nation in serving mankind. God has indeed been gracious.[10]

Of course, this outpouring of sentiment had to do with the forces of the Kaiser, not of Lenin. But the sentiment could easily be tailored to the latter. Whether Wilson really saw World War I as a gracious blessing of God, it is clear in retrospect that the appalling destruction resulting from four years of bloody conflict was hardly a glorious engagement. With over forty million dead and maimed in a war largely reflecting old, unnecessary antagonisms harking back to nineteenth-century monarchies, later generations would have some corrections to the Wilson vision. This is not to suggest that Wilson desired such a war. Indeed, he was elected in 1916 on the platform "He Kept Us Out of War." But the zealous pursuit of the idea of making the world safe for democracy led almost inevitably to a self-delusion respecting motives. Principles are better pursued with a realistic recognition of one's own flaws. Self-righteousness clouds vision at the most critical moments and often defeats the most noble of purposes.

A southern Calvinist minister, Joseph Wilson, reared young Woodrow to appreciate southern culture and religious traditions. The younger Wilson's deep sense of morality coupled with the Calvinistic understanding of a sovereign god undoubtedly found its origin in his father's sermons. In 1874 Woodrow wrote, "I am in my 17th year and it is sad, when looking over my past life, to see how few of those seventeen years I have spent in the fear of God, and how much time I have spent in the service of the Devil. . . . If God will give me the grace, I will try to serve him from this time on, and will."[11]

Wilson's sense of moral righteousness was combined, in the White House, with a conviction that America was the handmaiden of God designed to achieve divine purposes on earth. When he entered the presidency in 1913 he also possessed an unswerving belief in the free enterprise system. Long before politics touched his life, Wilson was driven by a strong moral sense. He was also seemingly unable to bear criticism. While a resident professor at Bryn Mawr College he wrote brief comments on the Washington political scene for *Bradstreets* in New York. On one occasion Mr. Bradstreet offered a bit of friendly criticism on Wilson's style. Wilson was so angered he nearly broke off the relationship.

Indeed, as a child Wilson was often chided by his father for his strong sense of pride. Of course Calvinists are supposed to subordinate personal pride, for which they normally take a great deal of self-satisfaction.

In any event, when Wilson became president he was prepared to view problems through moral spectacles. While he was a legitimate intellectual and scholar, nevertheless he was influenced heavily by his religious convictions and his understanding of the relationship between man and God. He saw God as an active participant in the historical process. In 1896 Wilson addressed the Princeton community, where he was then president. "There is nothing that gives such pith to public service as religion. A God of truth is no mean prompter to the enlightened service of mankind; and character formed as if in His eye has always a fibre and sanction such as you shall not obtain for the ordinary man from the mild promptings of philosophy."[12]

While Wilson's strong Presbyterianism was a part of his whole life, he was not altogether a narrow sectarian. "I believe," he wrote, "that too much effort is made to get people to believe for fear of the consequences of unbelief. I don't believe any man was ever drawn into heaven for fear he would go to hell. Because, if I understand the Scriptures in the least, they speak of a gospel of love. Except God draw you, you are not drawn."[13] On the other hand, Wilson was quite clearly agreeable to a form of predestination. He believed in the dynamic providence of God. He was certain that there was a moral direction in the universe. The Bible was his key. "A man has found himself when he has found his relation to the rest of the universe, and here is the book in which these relations are set forth."[14]

For Wilson Christianity was the one true faith. "Every thoughtful man born with a conscience must know a code of right and of pity to which he ought to conform; but without the motive of Christianity, without love, he may be the purest altruist and yet be as sad and as unsatisfied as Marcus Aurelius."[15] Wilson had no inkling of a problem in sending the following message to "soldiers and sailors of the United States." He wrote concerning Jesus as the Christ and concluded, "When you have read the Bible you will know that it is the Word of God, because you will have found it the key to your own heart, your own happiness, and your own duty."[16]

Two other examples from 1915 complete the picture of a man with a mission. "America has a great cause which is not confined to the American continent. It is the cause of humanity itself."[17] And in an address to the Federal Council of Churches on December 10, 1915, Wilson concluded his remarks about "A New Kind of Church Life" with the following admonition:

> The reason that I am proud to be an American is because America was given birth to by such conceptions as these; that its object in the world, its only reason for existence as a Government, was to show men the paths of liberty and of mutual service-ability, to lift the common man out of the paths, out of the sloughs of discouragement and even despair; set his feet upon firm ground; tell him, "Here is the high road upon which you are much entitled to walk as we are, and, we will see that there is a free field and no favor, and that as your moral qualities are and your physical powers so will your success be. We will not let any man make you afraid, and we will not let any man do you an injustice."[18]

The easy transfer of Wilson's mind from religious subjects to statecraft shows a remarkable sense of political ethics. While his presumptions are Christian, his moral code rather rigid, it is certainly the case that he frequently spoke as if he were translating his specific religious convictions into a humanistic ethic. Indeed, in the comment about Marcus Aurelius it seems clear that Wilson was quite prepared to find common ground with the non-Christian as long as there is a moral base for action. In this Wilson was distinctively beyond the narrow views of Luther and Calvin. With all his Christian commitment it is his translation of that into a moral crusade for the world that was problematic in 1918, and is even more so today.

World War I provided a platform upon which American democracy might at last be displayed. The resulting prestige and international power were, from the beginning, linked to a sense of divine mission. President Wilson was the primary architect of the linkage of Protestant Christianity with national goals.

The 1920s

As Wilson closed his presidency his optimism about Russia had been shattered by Communist success. Far from a fanatic on the question of domestic dangers posed by the rising tide of Marxism, he cautioned his attorney general, Mitchell Palmer, not to let the country "see red." Palmer defied the president and set about America's "red purge." Wilson did not cast the struggle against the Soviet Union in Christian vs. atheist terms, but he set the stage for such thinking by introducing his commitment to a messianic role for the United States in the world.

Warren Harding's most incisive religious observation while in the White House may have been, "God! what a job." As one biographer, Francis Russell observed, "Religion was for Harding like the Constitution, something to be honored and let alone. . . . There must be some reason for everything, he believed—in the odd moments when he thought about it—a God somewhere, an afterlife somehow in which one would not be judged too harshly for brass rails and poker games and the occasional midnight visits to the houses by the railroad station."[19] If Wilson's messianism was to take root in the White House it would have to wait for a time.

While presidents were ruminating with past traditions religion in America, particularly Protestantism, was in the midst of a major shift. Historian Robert T. Handy explored what he terms "The American Religious Depression, 1925-1935" in the journal *Church History*. Handy contends that by 1925 the Protestant churches were in a decline, witnessed to by a waning interest in the mission movement and in the optimism of the social gospel. Winthrop Hudson likewise identified this new mood. "Nothing is more striking than the astonishing reversal in the position occupied by the churches and the role played in American life which took place before the new century was well under way. By the nineteen twenties, the contagious enthusiasm . . . had largely evaporated."[20] Handy refers to a 1927 publication by Andre Siegfried that declared, "The civilization of the United States is essentially Protestant." As noted above, many historians have commented upon the almost total identification of Protestantism with Americanism in the nineteenth century. Sidney Mead observed in 1956 that, "We are still living with some of the results of this ideological amalgamation of evangelical Protestantism with Americanism."[21] According to Handy this alliance was reinforced in the early twenties. He argues further, "Protestantism entered the period of religious and economic depression as the dominant American religious tradition, closely identified with the culture." However, he notes, "Protestantism emerged from depression no longer in such a position; it was challenged by forces outside the Protestant churches and questioned by some within."[22]

The symbol of loss was the failure of prohibition legislation. As Handy says, "Prohibition itself was in one sense part of the struggle of country against city." So it was that the "final failure of prohibition made it clearer to many Protestants that the familiar American culture in which they had flourished and with which they had been so closely identified was going."[23] Response from the liberal pulpit of Harry Emerson Fosdick came in his admonition to "challenge" the prevailing culture. "What Christ does to modern culture is to challenge it."[24] Of course this was precisely what the fundamentalist Christians refused to do. Listening to Pat Buchanan or Cal Thomas berate the National Endowment for the Arts over what they perceive to be filth, one can hear the distant echo of the prohibitionist rhetoric.

Handy concludes his analysis, written in the year John Kennedy was elected, with these observations:

> During the period of religious and economic depression, then, the "Protestant era" in America was brought to a close; Protestantism emerged no longer as the "national religion." . . . The repudiation of the virtual identification of Protestantism with American culture by an able and growing group of religious leaders freed many Protestants to recover in a fresh way their own heritages and their original sources of inspiration. . . . In that period trends long in the making were dramatically revealed, and developments important to the future became visible.[25]

If we accept Handy's analysis of declining Protestantism beginning in 1925, President Coolidge was certainly an example. Coolidge was encapsulated in one of his few memorable remarks, "I have never been hurt by what I have not said." John Calvin Coolidge had a formless church background, though he attended a Congregational church in Massachusetts. He did not join a church in Washington while he was vice president, but upon assuming the presidency he joined the First Congregational Church. "Without fuss or publicity, he joined a church for the first time in his life."[26] William Allen White said he was a Calvinist and a Puritan.[27] His successor, Herbert Hoover, departed from fact, we imagine, when he quipped that Coolidge was "a fundamentalist in religion, in the economic and social order, and in fishing."[28] In sum, the most remarkable thing about the Coolidge years was not his religion but the national cult of the god of big business. Excessive emphasis on success in amassing material goods and its alliance with "good" religion was dominant. The social gospel of Walter Rauschenbusch was buried under the new "greenback gospel." One of the most popular books of the decade was Bruce Barton's *The Man Nobody Knows*, depicting Jesus as a topflight salesman and talented executive, molding twelve men into an all-time best management team.

Herbert Hoover was a religious man who recognized what he saw as a high responsibility to people. According to sociologist Digby Baltzell he "represented all the virtues of the last Anglo-Saxon-Protestant generation to dominate the American political establishment.[29] Hoover was a committed internationalist in his early years, but he had a constant fear of communism. He translated that into a dread of the New Deal as a collectivism headed toward its "bloody brother communism." As early as 1919 Hoover had used humanitarian concern over hunger in Russia as a means of forcing the Soviets to accept Western demands or starve. In 1950, shortly before his death, Hoover remained fixed on this conflict. "What the world needs today is a definite, spiritual mobilization of the nations who believe in God against this tide of Red agnosticism." He was certain that God would be with us in rejecting an atheistic other world.[30] As Hoover's years extended he grew more and more interested in invoking the Bible and the Christian faith, almost always in a crusade. Personally, he was a decent man, who could write in all seriousness, "The ethics of good sportsmanship are second only to religious ethics."[31] He was a most mannerly man.

The election of Franklin Roosevelt brought an Episcopalian pragmatist to the White House. His friend and speech writer, Judge Samuel Rosenman, offered one of the few personal glimpses into FDR's religious feelings.

> While the President was not a regular churchgoer, I always thought of him as a deeply religious man. . . . Roosevelt felt a veneration for his Creator which expressed itself often. . . . His references to God, so frequent in his speeches, came naturally to him; . . . I have often thought that his deep concern for his fellowmen—even those whom social and financial tradition might call the meanest and the lowliest—had its roots in his religious conviction of the innate dignity of every human being.[32]

Roosevelt's was a type of religious pragmatism that refused to identify deity as taking sides in political struggles. At the same time, Roosevelt was capable of drawing moral distinctions. Eleanor Roosevelt quoted here husband on this subject:

> I think it is unwise to say you do not believe in anything when you can't prove that it is either true or untrue. There is so much in the world which is always new in the way of discoveries that it is wiser to say that there may be spiritual things we are simply unable to fathom. Therefore I am interested and have respect for whatever people believe, even if I can not understand their beliefs or share their experiences.[33]

Reinhold Niebuhr, not always a friendly critic, but identified by George Kennan, speaking of the president's inner circle, as "father to us all," remarked of FDR, "He was a political liberal who subscribed to a hard-boiled pragmatism."[34] For Roosevelt there was no ritual of the past, no salvation for the future, only justice and freedom for the present. He was neither deity nor saint, but he comprehended the democracy he served in terms that the founders would have understood. "The fight for social justice and economic Democracy . . . is a long, weary, uphill struggle."

FDR's personal prestige lingered briefly after his death in 1945 before being buried under a barrage of political rhetoric. Republican revisionism made him a White House hero once more in the eighties and the Clinton years seem destined to restore much of the luster of FDR. On matters of church and state FDR's impact was, perhaps quite unwittingly, felt most dramatically in his appointment from 1937 to 1943 of Black, Frankfurter, Douglas, Jackson, and Rutledge to the Supreme Court bench.

Notes

1. "Letter of Madison to Jefferson, February 24, 1826," The Writings of James Madison, ed. Gaillard Hunt, vol. 9 (New York: G. P. Putnam's Sons, 1910), pp. 245–46. Of course Jefferson died on July 4 of that year.

2. U.S. Congress, Senate, Hearings before the Committee on the Judiciary, Prayer in Public Schools and Other Matters (Washington, D.C.: U.S. Government Printing Office, 1962), p. 55.

3. W. S. Hudson, ed., Nationalism and Religion in America (New York: Harper & Row, 1970), p. 120.

4. John Wilson, "Church and State in America," in James Madison on Religious Liberty, ed. Robert S. Alley (Buffalo, N.Y.: Prometheus

Books, 1985), p. 106.

5. Ibid., p. 108.

6. Louis Hartz, "The Nature of Revolution," *Hearings Before the Committee on Foreign Relations,* United States Senate, 90th Congress, 2nd Session (Feb. 26, 1968), p. 118.

7. Ibid.

8. *Address of the President of the United States, Delivered at a Joint Session of the Two Houses of Congress April 2, 1917,* published by Edward J. Clode, distributed by Grosset & Dunlap, 1917.

9. Ibid.

10. Edith Boling Wilson, ed., *Selected Literary and Political Papers and Addresses of Woodrow Wilson,* vol. 2 (New York: Grosset & Dunlap, 1927), p. 277.

11. Letters and papers of Woodrow Wilson to be found in the Woodrow Wilson Collection, Firestone Library, Princeton University.

12. Wilson Collection, Library of Congress.

13. E. B. Wilson, ed., *Selected Literary and Political Papers,* vol. 1, p. 183.

14. Ibid., p. 344.

15. Woodrow Wilson, *When a Man Comes to Himself* (New York: Harper & Brothers, 1901), p. 20.

16. *Congressional Record,* vol. 55, p. 6041.

17. E. B. Wilson, ed., "Address to the Daughters of the American Revolution, Oct. 11, 1915," *Selected Literary and Political Papers,* p. 134.

18. *Congressional Record,* vol. 53, pp. 15751-53.

19. Francis Russell, *The Shadow of Blooming Grove: Warren G. Harding in His Times* (New York: McGraw-Hill Book Co., 1968), pp. 168-69.

20. Winthrop Hudson, *The Great Tradition of the American Churches* (New York: Harper and Bros., 1953), p. 196.

21. Sidney Mead, "American Protestantism Since the Civil War. From Denominationalism to Americanism," *Journal of Religion* 36 (1956): 1.

22. Robert T. Handy, "The American Religious Depression, 1925-1935," *Church History* 29 (1960): 3-16.

23. Ibid.

24. Harry Emerson Fosdick, "Beyond Modernism: A Sermon," *The Christian Century* 52 (1935): 1552.

25. Handy, "American Religious Depression," p. 16.

26. Donald R. McCoy, *Calvin Coolidge: The Quiet President* (New York: Macmillan, 1967), p. 150.

27. William Allen White, *A Puritan in Babylon: The Story of Calvin Coolidge* (New York: Macmillan, 1939), p. 14.

28. Herbert Hoover, *The Memoirs of Herbert Hoover, 1920-33* (New York: Macmillan, 1952), p. 56.

29. E. Digby Baltzell, *The Protestant Establishment: Aristocracy and Caste in America* (New Haven: Yale University Press, 1987), p. 227.

30. Herbert Hoover, *Addresses upon the American Road, 1948-50* (Stanford, Calif.: Stanford University Press, 1951), p. 66.

31. Ibid., p. 175.

32. Samuel I. Rosenman, *Working With Roosevelt* (New York: Harper, 1952), p. 433.

33. Eleanor Roosevelt, *That I Remember* (New York: Harper, 1949), p. 341.

34. *The New York Times,* June 3, 1971, p. 43.

5

From *Cantwell* to *Everson:* 1940 to 1947

We turn now to the events in the Supreme Court that set the stage for the critical opinion of the Court in 1947, *Everson v. Board of Education.* The most important pre-1940s case came in 1925 when the Court in *Pierce* v. *Society of Sisters* ruled that an Oregon law requiring attendance at public schools could not prohibit a private alternative. The case was decided on Fourteenth Amendment grounds and became what has been termed the Magna Carta of parochial schools. Five years later in *Cochran* v. *Board of Education* the Court upheld a Louisiana law providing textbooks to parochial school children, again on Fourteenth Amendment grounds that otherwise persons would be deprived of property without due process.

Conscientious objection became the focus of two cases, *United States v. Schwimmer* (1929) and *United States v. Macintosh* (1931), in which the issue was clearly drawn between Justice George Sutherland, writing for the majority, and Justice Charles Evans Hughes for the minority of four. Sutherland stated, "When he speaks of putting his allegiance to the will of God above his allegiance to the government, it is evident . . . tnat he means to make his own interpretation of the will of God the decisive test which shall conclude the government and stay its hand." Responding, Hughes noted, "There is abundant room for enforcing the requisite authority of law as it is enacted and requires obedience, and for maintaining the conception of the supremacy of law as essential to orderly government, without demanding that either citizens or applicants for citizenship shall assume by oath to regard allegiance to God as subordinate to civil power." Both cases dealt with prospective immigrants. In 1934 the Court, without dissent, upheld a California law requiring students at a state university to "take a course in military science and tactics." Again, the case was brought on Fourteenth Amendment grounds.[1]

Since 1940, when the Supreme Court in *Cantwell* v. *Connecticut* first applied the religion clauses of the First Amendment to state legislation by incorporating the Fourteenth Amendment, there has been a steady flow of cases considered for adjudication by the justices. In the past fifty years nearly all the decisions related to the clauses have involved either local or state laws.

This would have come as no surprise to James Madison. As noted earlier, while leading the forces favorable to an amendment on religious freedom in the 1789 Congress Madison supported applying what was to become the First Amendment to the states. He conceived this to be "the most valuable amendment on the whole list; if there was any reason to restrain the government of the United States from infringing upon these essential rights, it was equally necessary that they should be secured against the state governments; he thought that if they provided against the one, it was as necessary to provide against the other, and was satisfied that it would be equally grateful to the people."[2]

Madison frequently alluded to the role of factions in maintaining the rights of citizens. He often warned of the danger inherent in the tyranny of a majority. At the federal level the balance of those factions offered a far greater protection of individual rights than did the more homogeneous cultures in the individual states. It is important to remember that several states retained religious establishments well after 1789. With few exceptions the principles Madison espoused prevented any frontal assault upon free exercise of religion at the national level. But, as has been observed, the nineteenth century offers ample evidence of the Protestant hegemony that dominated politics in the states.

In Congress Protestant pluralism was a significant factor early in its history. As the nation grew and diversified it was the Congress that first reflected the changing patterns. It has been federalism that has overcome, on a consistent basis, the provincialism of states, individually or in concert. In its earliest free exercise case, *Reynolds* v. *United States* (1879), the Supreme Court upheld federal laws forbidding bigamy in the territories. Chief Justice Morrison Remick Waite wrote for the Court, asserting, "Congress was deprived of all legislative power over mere opinion, but was left free to reach actions which were in violation of social duties or subversive of good order" (p. 353).

Occasionally, as in the case of conscientious objection in the 1960s and the issue of wearing religious garb in the armed services, the Court has addressed congressional actions that involved free exercise rights. The vast majority of the cases since 1940 have, however, been concerned with state or local laws.

That was made possible by the 1940 decision in *Cantwell*, in which Justice Owen Roberts wrote for the Court, "The First Amendment declares that Congress shall make no law respecting an establishment of religion or prohibiting the free exercise thereof. *The Fourteenth Amendment has rendered the legislatures of the states as incompetent as Congress to enact such laws*" (emphasis added).

Notes

1. *Hamilton v. Regents of University of California,* 293 US 245 (1934).
2. *Congressional Register,* II, 227 for August 17, 1789.

6

From *Everson* to JFK: 1947 to 1960

Religion in Public Schools: *Everson* and *McCollum*

The Supreme Court created instant historical precedent when, in 1947, it found in favor of the state of New Jersey in the *Everson* case. Despite the narrow margin, five to four, all the justices apparently were in full agreement with the principles enunciated in Justice Hugo Black's majority opinion. He wrote:

> The "establishment of religion" clause of the First Amendment means at least this: Neither a state nor the Federal Government can set up a church. Neither can pass laws which aid one religion, aid all religions, or prefer one religion over another. Neither can force nor influence a person to go to or to remain away from church against his will or force him to profess a belief or disbelief in any religion. No person can be punished for entertaining or professing religious beliefs or disbeliefs, for church attendance or non-attendance. No tax in any amount, large or small, can be levied to support any religious activities

or institutions, whatever they may be called, or whatever form they may adopt to teach or practice religion. Neither a state nor the Federal Government can, openly or secretly, participate in the affairs of any religious organizations or groups and vice versa. In the words of Jefferson, the clause against establishment of religion by law was intended to erect "a wall of separation between Church and State."[1]

The thing that divided the justices was a quite narrow interpretation of what has been called the "child benefit theory." Black and his colleagues separated the child's interest in this case from the First Amendment issues and upheld the state's right to fund transportation to parochial schools. While some advocates of broader aid to church schools took heart at the majority opinion, it soon became clear that the decision did not rest on the child's right to an education but, rather, the child's right to safety. Basing their interpretation of the religion clauses firmly in the Madison/Jefferson tradition, all nine justices created a firm separationist view in 1947.

There was some grumbling from citizen groups that agreed with the minority, but by and large the decision raised little uproar. A year later one can detect a shift in public response to this new area of judicial review. It had to do with the Court's decision rendered on March 8, 1948, in *McCollum* v. *Board of Education*. By an eight-to-one margin the justices found that public schools in Champaign, Illinois, had violated the establishment clause by permitting religious groups to use classrooms during school hours for the teaching of religion.

At the time of the finding by the Court the Senate was in the process of considering a federal aid to education bill. Its sponsor, Sen. Robert Taft of Ohio, informed the Senate that *McCollum* "makes it almost impossible for any state to give aid to any school except possibly by bus transportation." It was early evidence that construction of federal legislation would frequently be affected by Court decisions, sometimes to comply, often to defy.

One of the most distinguished scholars to challenge McCollum was theologian Reinhold Niebuhr. In a column entitled "Secularism and Religion in Education," he wrote that many Protestants "do not seem to realize that if the separation of Church and State is made absolute, education, and indeed our culture in general, must become secular." For Niebuhr the decision "embodies a philosophy in which the secular idea that religion is dangerous to the peace and unity of a community becomes compounded with certain Protestant notions that religion is purest when it is most private." His fear was either creation of a complete vacuum regarding ultimate issues of the meaning of life or a secularized form of religious faith.[2]

While Illinois officials sought to comply with the Court's action, church groups in other states defied the ruling. The Virginia Council of Churches continued to press its own teaching of religion in public schools in the face of State Attorney General J. Lindsay Almond's observation that "I have grave doubts as to the constitutionality of any plan operating" so that school authorities were "responsible . . . for the discipline of the child."[3]

Almost immediately an alternative plan was attempted in several localities. In Champaign religion classes held after school hours appeared to meet with success. In fact the chief instructor for the city's Council for Religious Education said the new idea had met with sufficient support to "warrant starting others next year in the adjoining city of Urbana."[4] In 1952 in *Zorach* v. *Clauson* the justices by a six-to-three majority found a "released time" formula constitutional. Justice William Douglas asserted that expanding *McCollum* to apply in the Zorach case would endorse "a philosophy of hostility to religion." Justice Robert Jackson, in a biting dissent, wrote that "the McCollum case has passed like a storm in a teacup. . . . Today's judgment will be more interesting to students of psychology and of the judicial process than to students of constitutional law."

The Truman and Eisenhower Years

In spite of the sharp exchange between justices in the McCollum case, public discussion of church/state court decisions was quite muted. The one major area of national debate had to do with public funding for parochial schools, an issue as yet unattended by the Supreme Court. The country was quickly gripped by the realities of the cold-war conflict with the Soviets. That in turn plunged the United States into a massive red scare that affected everything from the academy of learning to the Academy of Motion Picture Arts and Sciences. The names of Richard Nixon and Joseph McCarthy became synonymous with anti-red activity. President Truman was no slacker in those days of nearly uncontrolled fear.

In that period there was evident a national focus upon religion. Mainline Protestant leaders held preaching missions across the land; Bishop Fulton Sheen became a Roman Catholic guru to the millions who turned to the television set in the early fifties; and Billy Graham rose to become an icon, the guru of godly mayhem directed at communism. Early in the fifties Graham thrust the deity into the fray, asserting that America was God's chosen nation.

Harry Truman had been reared in accordance with typical patterns of the Midwest which had its own peculiar religious heritage. He imbibed a religious tradition woven into the cultural fabric. In most small towns during Truman's youth Protestant churches dominated the mores of the community. The Trumans moved to Independence, Missouri, when Harry was six. According to his *Memoirs* his parents decided the children should attend Sunday school. The Presbyterian church they chose was a kind of social center. Married in an Episcopal church, Truman's Baptist connection was of adult origin.

As president, Truman was likely affected by a heritage that perceived Christianity as America's religion. In his 1949 inaugural he spoke of the "false philosophy" of communism as opposite to the moral uprightness of democracy. He called for a national crusade for freedom grounded in a dichotomy between two world ideologies. "With God's help the future of mankind will be assured in a world of justice, harmony, and peace."[5]

Truman, toward the close of his years in office, saw the development of an unbridled ideological warfare that he was powerless to contain. Distinguished columnist Walter Lippmann supported Eisenhower in 1952 because he believed only a Republican could halt the demagogic Sen. Joseph McCarthy.

Truman regularly injected religion into policy. By 1949 his religious zeal had become too much for the *Christian Century*. Truman asserted, in a speech to a group of Episcopal bishops, that America was living by the Sermon on the Mount. The *Century* noted that the president might consider pardoning imprisoned conscientious objectors since we were living by that sermon.[6] Truman pressed on, asserting that communists were evil because they did not believe in a supreme being. After the November election of 1952 Truman spoke to a group of churchmen. "Democracy is, first and foremost, a spiritual force, it is built upon a spiritual basis—and on a belief in God and an observance of moral principles. And in the long run only the church can provide that basis. Our founders knew this truth—and we will neglect it at our peril."[7] A year earlier he had expressed similar sentiments. "Our religious faith gives us the answer to the false beliefs of Communism. . . . I have the feeling that God has created us and brought us to our present position of power and strength for some great purpose."[8]

Truman was neither the first nor last to employ religious language to accomplish political ends. But these gods have come in many manifestations. Who is the true god of America? Is she the elective god of judgment affirmed by Wilson? Is he the god of business rewarding the practice of diligence as defined by Hoover? Is she the god of the universe whose benevolent plan may inspire all men and women as it did Franklin Roosevelt? Is he the friendly sovereign who has chosen America, blessed her, and given her a special mission as suggested by Truman, Eisenhower, Reagan, and Bush? Just how is America to find its way through the theological thickets of her variegated religious heritage? Politicians seldom bother themselves about such questions. The Supreme Court was unable to avoid them as it undertook the adjudication of establishment and free exercise disputes. In its role as interpreter of the nation's political "scripture," the Constitution, the Court will inevitably create tension with citizens and their representatives when it hands down "final" decisions that seem at odds with some reigning popular religion.

In the election of Dwight Eisenhower Americans turned to a man who seemed to incarnate their corporate notion of deity. Religion was everywhere in the fifties. Will Herberg commented:

> But it is a curious kind of religion. The very same people who are so unanimous in identifying themselves religiously, who are joining churches at an accelerated rate, and who take it for granted that religion is a "very important" thing, do not hesitate to acknowledge that religion is quite peripheral to their

everyday lives; more than half of them quite frankly admit that their religious beliefs have no influence whatever on their ideas in economics and politics, and a good proportion of the remainder are obviously uncertain.[9]

It was a time when laymen became bold to scold the clergy for involving itself in matters other than spiritual, i.e., politics and social justice.

Shortly after his election Eisenhower said, "Our government makes no sense unless it is founded in a deeply felt religious faith, and I don't care what it is." He expressed a similar attitude in 1948. "I am the most intensely religious man I know. . . . Nobody goes through six years of war without faith. That does not mean that I adhere to any sect. A democracy cannot exist without a religious base. I believe in democracy."[10] Working from that concept, Eisenhower wanted to rally all faiths to endorse the American system as God's system. Sociologist Digby Baltzell was quite correct in remarking, "President Eisenhower calmly reigned as representative of a generation still dominated by the Protestant establishment."[11]

Ike was an almost perfect mirror of a domestic move to piety that identified America with some nebulous deity. On the Sunday following his inauguration Eisenhower joined a sect, the Presbyterian Church. It was a Protestant middle way for Ike who, according to the *Chicago Tribune,* received baptism. Paul Hutchinson observed that he was "fervent about vague religion."[12] This was amply demonstrated in his remarks about religious music. "There was a song some years ago that made a great impression on me, and it has a title that has been rather a motto for me ever since I got into politics. And it was this: 'I Believe.' "[13] In reality this was faith in belief, an affirmation of cause and effect— "For every drop of rain that falls, a flower grows."

The high priests of popular religion in the fifties were Norman Vincent Peale and Billy Graham. Eisenhower was comfortable with both men. It was Ike who inaugurated the White House prayer breakfast and who tried to establish a national day of prayer. Commentator Elmer Davis remarked that religion and recreation were not far apart for the president. On July 4, 1953, Eisenhower called the nation to its knees in prayer. On that day he went fishing in the morning, golfing in the afternoon, and played bridge in the evening. Eisenhower opened Cabinet meetings with prayer. He became, for millions of citizens, the center of piety for America. The president made the nation feel good. He was roundly praised for supporting the addition of "under God" to the Pledge of Allegiance. This was accomplished by legislation written by Rep. Louis Rabaut of Michigan during the eighty-third Congress. Definition of this amorphous deity was seen as unnecessary, perhaps because it would have been near impossible.

Billy Graham made no secret of his uneasiness with Truman. After Ike's election Graham asserted, "The overwhelming majority of the American people felt a little more secure realizing that we have a man who believes in prayer at the helm of our government at this crucial hour."[14] The administration championed a domestic "Goldilocks Era"—one where everything was "just right."

The gloss of the godly leadership should not hide the essential ingredient of legalism buried deep within the traditions espoused by Eisenhower, encouraged by Graham, and exported by John Foster Dulles, the secretary of state. Dulles, a professional diplomat, came to Washington with a long history of association with the Protestant ecumenical movement. His Presbyterian faith was, in many ways, similar to that of Woodrow Wilson, but it drove him to far more rigid foreign policy. Charles West commented in 1958:

> Mr. Dulles belongs to the company of those whose anti-Com-
> munism is a matter of absolute principle, not of practical realism,
> because his own faith is so closely bound up with the ideals
> of the American tradition. . . . He fails to perceive the relativity
> of these ideals. . . . this failure of insight is rooted in a faith
> which emphasizes the Law at the expense of the Gospel.[15]

Dulles appeared to equate western Christianity, particularly in the United States, with the deity's will. By injecting a doctrinaire, either-or mentality into his policies, Dulles contributed to a surly mood in the nation toward even the slightest socialist tinted idea. This was transferred to many churches during that era.

To his credit, Dulles found no merit in McCarthy's tactics. He transcended them in his arena. Eisenhower, perhaps taking a cue from his secretary, tried the same thing, but with little success. Finally McCarthy, embittered by his crushing defeat in the Army/McCarthy hearings, attacked five thousand Protestant clergy as "red" or "pink." This gave the president the high ground. Richard Nixon was given the "opportunity" to axe the senator. In the final analysis, McCarthyism was too brash and harsh for the "man upstairs" mentality that settled over the nation by mid-decade. However, at the same time Dulles's hard-line foreign policy exacerbated relations with potential friends in the emerging Third World.

Eisenhower's popularity did not come from intellect or commitment to a cause. Unlike FDR, Ike did not move the country to reflect his personality. Rather, Eisenhower reflected back to the people their own popular image of one nation under God. He possessed a generalized piety that made millions feel good. He brought that piety to the Potomac.[16] Will Herberg was on the mark in noting that Eisenhower represented the secular religionist "being serious about religion but not taking religion seriously." That could equally be said of Graham and Peale. In that mood the nation may have moved closer than ever to establishing a kind of civil religion. Had it happened it would have been of a modified Puritan variety, spouting many legalisms but divested of ethical or theological content. It was a decade of simplistic faith when Hollywood peddled *Peter Marshall* and audiences responded with tears and "faith." It was a nostalgic look back at the old time religion.

The calm of domestic tranquility, so consistently portrayed on television by the "Leave It To Beaver" and "Father Knows Best" television series, was in marked contrast to the violence emerging around the world. The 1950s not only produced the irrational behavior of McCarthyism, it was frequently consumed with public fear over the Bomb, with late night talk show conversations about bomb shelters. The launch of Sputnik in 1957 shattered illusions about American scientific superiority. And hovering over the domestic landscape was the anger engendered by the 1954 Supreme Court decision in *Brown* v. *Board of Education.* In spite of Truman's religious doctrine, the Sermon on the Mount was generally ignored by white citizens in the wake of that landmark case. An entire generation of young Americans, black and white, were sentenced before their birth to racial animosity and suspicion. The unholy roll call of the fifties includes George Wallace, Harry Byrd, Orval Faubus, Strom Thurmond, and Ross Barnette, ably abetted by J. Edgar Hoover. That tight southern political alliance against the Court resulted in lost opportunities and lost children. The decade of the fifties may rank as the time of the greatest irresponsibility in our history. In spite of all the good will manifest in the character of Martin Luther King, Jr., so movingly expressed in his letter from the Birmingham jail, a deaf ear was turned by white politicians who, a decade later, would be in a lather over public school prayer.

Nothing in our recent past so clearly identifies the shallowness of the public religious sentiments of the era than does the fundamentally unjust treatment of black citizens. And the nation would listen in vain for years to hear a mumbling word on the subject from Billy Graham. In light of these facts it was fortunate for advocates of genuine adherence to the religion clauses of the First Amendment that no controversial cases related to them appeared in the fifties.

In 1953 President Eisenhower appointed Earl Warren as Chief Justice of the Supreme Court. By 1954 he appears to have regretted the choice. But in addition to matters having to do with segregation, the Court was quietly building an effective philosophical base for a series of establishment clause cases that would, in 1962, result in a confrontation in which almost all of those fifties public religious manifestations would be marshalled against the Warren Court. But even though a firestorm of protest resulted from the *Engel* decision, the historical timing was fortuitous. The Court was to be emphatically supported in its school prayer decisions by the new president, John F. Kennedy, the first Roman Catholic to hold the office.

Notes

1. *Everson v. Board of Education,* 330 US 1 (1947). See Justice Black's opinion for the court.

2. Reinhold Niebuhr, "Secularism and Religion in Education," copyright by Religious News Service, 1948. It should not be assumed that Niebuhr was in the camp with those who saw the United States as a Christian nation. In a column just two weeks earlier, "The False Hope of National Messianism," Niebuhr wrote, "The idea that a single nation has the one special gift, required for the redemption of the world, is from the Christian standpoint, the final form of sinful pride."

3. Religious News Service report in the *Religious Herald*, July 22, 1948, p. 3.

4. See Religious News Service report in the *Religious Herald*, May 20, 1948, p. 3.

5. Harry S. Truman, *Memoirs: Years of Decision*, vol. 1 (Garden City, N.Y.: Doubleday, 1955), p. 419.

6. "Truman Calls Sermon on Mount Our Guide," editorial, *The Christian Century* 66, no. 38 (September 21, 1949): p. 1091.

7. *Public Papers of the President of the United States: Harry S. Truman—1952* (Washington, D.C.: U.S. Government Printing Office, 1966), p. 1063.

8. *Public Papers of the President of the United States: Harry S. Truman—1951* (Washington, D.C.: U.S. Government Printing Office, 1966), pp. 210, 548-49.

9. Will Herberg, "Religion and Culture in Present-Day America," in Irwin Unger, David Brody, and Paul Goodman, eds., *The Record of American History*, vol. 2 (Waltham, Mass.: Xerox College Publishing, 1971), p. 448. Stephen L. Carter's *The Culture of Disbelief* (New York: Basic Books, 1993), while addressing what he perceives as modern trivializing of religious devotion, failed to examine the fities as a prime example of precisely that trivializing process.

10. Ibid.

11. E. Digby Baltzell, *The Protestant Establishment* (New Haven: Yale University Press, 1987), p. 296.

12. Paul Hutchinson, "The President's Religious Faith," *The Christian Century* 71, no. 12 (March 24, 1954): 362.

13. "The President Believes," editorial, *The Christian Century* 75, no. 46 (November 12, 1958): 1294.

14. William McLoughin, *Billy Graham: Revivalist in a Secular Age* (New York: Ronald Press, 1969), p. 117.

15. Charles C. West, *Communism and the Theologians* (Philadelphia: Westminster Press, 1958), p. 40.

16. William Lee Miller, *Piety Along the Potomac: Notes on Politics and Morals in the Fifties* (Boston: Houghton Mifflin, 1964).

7

Engel, Schempp, and Aftermath: 1962-63

On January 28, 1992, the United States Senate by a vote of thirty-eight to fifty-five defeated a school prayer amendment offered by Sen. Jesse Helms, which he sought to attach to an education bill. The vote came a little less than five months shy of the thirtieth anniversary of the decision by the Supreme Court in *Engel* v. *Vitale,* which declared prescribed public school prayers unconstitutional. In those three decades there has been an unending stream of legislative maneuverings aimed at undermining that landmark decision. Of all the Court rulings of this century none has sparked more action in Congress than *Engel.* The testimony on the subject fills volumes of committee hearing publications.

The public outrage stirred by the decision led to a new round of highway billboards calling for Chief Justice Earl Warren's impeachment. Almost immediately a myth was spread across the nation insisting that the Court had "kicked God out of the schools." It was a theme adopted by religious figures such as Norman Vincent Peale and Billy Graham, both of whom urged quick congressional action to counter the Court. Both houses of

Congress began committee hearings and floor amendments that have persisted through the administrations of seven presidents. The last extensive Senate inquiry occurred in 1983, when the Committee on the Judiciary's Subcommittee on the Constitution held three days of hearings in April, May, and June, producing 773 pages of testimony.

Arguments in the *Engel* case took place on April 3, 1962. While it addressed a twenty-two-word prayer—"Almighty God, we acknowledge our dependence upon Thee, and we beg Thy blessing upon us, our parents, our teachers, and our country"— approved by the New York State Board of Regents for use in public school classrooms, similar practices were in place through- out the nation. In the District of Columbia the school board directed that school sessions should be opened with "the salute to the flag, a reading from the Bible without note or comment, and the Lord's Prayer." The superintendent of the school urged the school board to continue the practice in the face of a protest from the Jewish Community Council of Greater Washington.[1] By October the American Civil Liberties Union had entered this dispute, demanding that recitation of the Lord's Prayer be dis- continued immediately.[2]

On June 25, 1962, the Court ruled the Regents' prayer uncon- stitutional, setting loose a firestorm of protest across the nation. Addressing a session of the National Catholic Laymen's Retreat Conference in Portland, Sen. Eugene McCarthy said of the Supreme Court justices, "It was the only thing they [the Court] could do." He went on to comment on the heated response of some of his congressional colleagues. "Some genuinely believed it was an incorrect decision. . . . Others were critical to bolster their attack on the Court for its desegregation decisions. . . . Others were just 'demagoguing.' "[3] It is fair to say that the second reason was quite significant among Southern conservatives who were still engaged in delaying tactics related to *Brown v. Board of Education.* Those same elected officials represented a constituency that was heavily weighted with conservative Protestant religious traditions. While protesting desegregation often proved difficult to embrace in a nation whose conscience had been affected by the protests and the ringing words of Martin Luther King, Jr., this new issue might well place those politicians on a presumed high moral ground against a perceived secularistic trend in the Court.

In the two weeks following the *Engel* decision the *New York Times* recorded a series of negative reactions. Representative George Andrews of Alabama said, "They put the Negroes in the schools and now they've driven God out." Congressman John Rooney of New York warned "that the ruling could put the United States schools on the same basis as Russian schools." Cardinal Spellman said, "I am shocked and frightened that the Supreme Court has declared unconstitutional a simple and voluntary declaration of belief in God by public school children." His counterpart in Los Angeles, Cardinal McIntyre asserted, "The decision is positively shocking and scandalizing to one of American blood and principles." Billy Graham was "shocked and disappointed . . . another step toward secularism in the United States."[4]

The following day Rep. Frank Becker of New York called the decision "the most tragic in the history of the United States." Rep. John Bell Williams of Mississippi saw it as "a deliberate and carefully planned conspiracy to substitute materialism for spiritual values." Senator Prescott Bush of Connecticut felt the decision was "unfortunate, divisive and quite unnecessary." And that bastion of virtue, Senator Herman Talmadge of Georgia said it was "an outrageous edict which has numbed the conscience and shocked the highest sensibilities of the nation."

Clerics continued a bombardment with Cardinal Cushing of Boston saying the decision was "fuel for Communist propaganda."

An editorial in *The Pilot,* the oldest Catholic paper in the country, informed its readers that it "is a stupid decision, a doctrinaire decision, an unrealistic decision, a decision that spits in the face of our history, our tradition and our heritage as a religious people"[5]

A reasoned response came from the White House when President John Kennedy in a news conference said, "We have in this case a very easy remedy, and that is to pray ourselves. And I would think that it would be a welcome reminder to every American family that we can pray a good deal more at home, we can attend our churches with a good deal more fidelity, and we can make the true meaning of prayer much more important in the lives of all our children." On another political front the Alabama legislature approved a resolution denouncing the decision as a "diabolical" departure from the American way of life. It called for a constitutional amendment to override the Court.[6]

One voice that was heard in those early days after the decision is particularly interesting. Senator Sam Ervin of North Carolina said, "I should like to ask whether we would be far wrong in saying that in this decision the Supreme Court has held that God is unconstitutional and for that reason the public schools must be segregated against Him?"[7] Within a short period of years the senator would become one of the chief advocates on behalf of the Court's interpretations of the religion clauses.

By mid-July the rush of statements declined but still there were serious charges made by respected clergy. On July 12 Episcopal Bishop James A. Pike addressed a men's club in San Francisco, informing them that the Court had "just deconsecrated the nation."

In early July the New York Board of Regents urged school systems in the state to recognize the Court decision as the law of the land. It asserted that teachers could still stress "fundamental values." Gov. Nelson Rockefeller also said the schools should adhere to the Court's decision. The New York response was in marked contrast with other events of the summer. At the annual governor's conference in Hershey, Pennsylvania, an amendment to the Constitution that would permit voluntary prayer in the nation's public schools was called for with only Rockefeller abstaining. He took the unusual position that the "Court's decision should be thoroughly studied before action was taken."

In that same month Rep. Eugene Siler of Kentucky suggested to Congress the adoption of a "Christian amendment" to the Constitution that would curb the *Engel* decision. According to news reports in July there was a rush by members of Congress to introduce over twenty-five different resolutions proposing constitutional amendments to override the Court's decision. The National Education Association, meeting in Denver that same month, refused to commend the Court decision. Instead a resolution was passed calling for a year-long study of the full impact of *Engel*. In contrast, the Vermont State Board of Education passed a resolution expressing the feeling that the "intermingling of religious expressions and practices in tax supported educational institutions is consistent with the federal Constitution."[8]

Senate Judiciary Committee Hearings, 1962

A month after the *Engel* decision the Senate held hearings for two days. Disjointed and with little evidence of direction, the Committee on the Judiciary, under the direction of Sen. Olin Johnston, due to the absence of the chairman, Sen. James Eastland, met on July 26 and again on August 2.[9]

The Committee had five proposals for consideration:
S.J. Res. [Senate Joint Resolution] 205—Proposing an

amendment to the Constitution to permit the offering of prayer in public schools;

S.J. Res. 206—Proposing an amendment to the Constitution to permit the use of prayer in public schools;

S.J. Res. 207—Proposing an amendment to the Constitution permitting the offering of prayers and the reading of the Bible in public schools in the United States, and relating to the right of a state to enact legislation on the basis of its own public policy on questions of decency and morality;

S. Con. Res. 81—That it is the sense of Congress that the designation by a public school authority of a nonsectarian prayer does not constitute an establishment of religion;

S. Res. 356—Providing any public school system may provide time during the school day for prayerful meditation.

While Sen. Johnston stated that it was the intention of the committee "to hear as many . . . witnesses as possible," in fact only proponents of the resolutions appeared before the committee, with those opposed relegated to filing statements.

The first witness was Sen. Kenneth Keating of New York. He saw the Court as "putting a new gloss on the First Amendment under which every public or governmental manifestation of kinship with religion will be in jeopardy." However, unlike many of his colleagues, particularly those from the South, Keating reminded his peers, "One can disagree with a decision of the Court without impugning the motives, integrity of [or] good faith of the Justices of our High Tribunal. Vituperative denunciations of the Court or any of its members is out of harmony with the subject matter of our concern and will completely discredit attempts to modify or clarify the Court's decision."

Interestingly, the first critic outside the Senate to be cited was Art Carney, the television actor, who wrote in part, "To pray is to communicate with God. If this is made unconstitutional in any area of the lives of Americans, we feel our country is in jeopardy."

The next witness was Sen. John Stennis of Mississippi, sponsor of S.J. Res. 206. His purpose was to amend the Constitution to "provide that it shall not be construed to prohibit non-denominational religious observances through prayers, . . ."[10] Sen. Willis Robertson, father of faith healer Pat Robertson, followed with similar pleas for passage of an amendment, adding a lengthy historical analysis that he felt supported his opposition. It is particularly interesting how he focused upon the concurring opinion of Justice William O. Douglas in *Engel* in an effort to discredit the Court's decision. There followed Sens. Vance Hartke of Indiana and Beall of Maryland, who supported other plans of attack on the Court decision.

Then the committee heard from Rep. Eugene Siler of Kentucky who asserted, "We believe that what our Constitution needs is a fundamental change, something to guide all our courts in these different areas, and we believe we have it in the proposed Christian amendment which has been introduced by nine of us over in the House, and which has been introduced in five different Congresses here in the Senate."[11] Siler was referring to an amendment first introduced by the Judiciary Committee in the Senate in 1934. He reintroduced that amendment:

Section 1. This Nation devoutly recognizes the authority and laws of Jesus Christ, Saviour and Ruler of Nations, through whom are bestowed the blessings of Almighty God.

Section 2. This amendment shall not be interpreted so as to result in the establishment of any particular ecclesiastical organization or in the abridgment of the rights of religious freedom, or freedom of speech or press or of peaceful assemblage.

Section 3. Congress shall have power in such cases as it

may deem proper to provide a suitable oath or affirmation for citizens whose religious scruples prevent them from giving unqualified allegiance to the Constitution as herein amended.

While this was perhaps the most bizarre of the suggestions placed before the Congress in the thirty years following *Engel,* the theme of a Christian nation was not new. We have already encountered it in the writing of Justice Story. And it would reappear in the utterances of various religious figures such as Billy Graham, Jerry Falwell, and Pat Robertson in the years following 1962.

The next witness was Sen. Strom Thurmond of South Carolina. He raised the states rights issue and then went about the task of demonstrating that *Engel* "would be, in effect, the establishment of atheism as our officially recognized religion."[12] The main thrust of Senate Resolution 81 seemed to be the prologue in which Sens. Thurmond and Robertson decried the atheist efforts to eliminate recognition of God as they insisted that "the greatest threat to our political and religious freedom is posed by nations who deny the existence of God."[13]

The committee met for a second time on August 2. First it heard more testimony from Sens. Robertson and Stennis. Robertson was present to endorse a proposal to be offered that morning by Bishop James A. Pike, Episcopal bishop of the diocese of California. Sen. Stennis concurred. Senator Hart, who was presiding, seemed almost obsequious as he urged Bishop Pike to "feel free to read" his statement "in any manner you choose, interrupting yourself, adding comments as you go along." In sum, "Please feel free to present your statement in any form." This is a far cry from the carefully defined restrictions normally applied to witnesses before committees. It is important to note that at the time Pike was a religious celebrity who was frequently in the headlines. His generally liberal image probably gave him a special value to the proponents of constitutional amendments.

Pike began by grandly assuming that he and a handful of senators were gathered that day "to go further" with the Founders' work "to achieve their intentions."[14] He then rang the changes on the popular theme of the southern senators, states rights. Speaking of the Tenth Amendment, Pike said, "I might remind the distinguished Senators that this, in short, is our States rights amendment." He insisted that the Supreme Court was in error in church-state matters stemming from the *Cantwell* decision of 1940. Nevertheless, Pike accepted that this interpretation was not likely to be reversed so he moved to an original intent argument on establishment. But he had built his bridges to a number of segregationist senators in the bargain.

Asked whether the New York prayer put an undue burden on those who did not wish to pray, Pike turned the argument adroitly: "In the mentality of the kids, I have four children, and sometimes the ability to be nonconformist is a great delight. I know some kinds of young people who would just love to have permission to walk out at that point."

It is important to recognize how amendment proponents continued to refer to Justice Douglas and his assertion that by logic there should be no paid chaplain in the Congress. Dismissing the remaining justices they used the Douglas demurrer as almost a badge of honor. "But Mr. Justice Black groups your prayers and that of the Supreme Court as patriotic ceremonial goings-on; actually I think in logic, Mr. Justice Douglas is right," said Bishop Pike.

In the discussion with Pike it appears that he and Sen. Robertson came to an agreement that a constitutional amendment was needed and that its purpose would be to define the meaning of "establishment" in the First Amendment. Pike suggested it be defined as "the recognition as an established church of any denomination, sect, or organized religious association."[15] Such a definition would, it was assumed, eliminate decisions like *Engel* since a prayer was neither a church, denomination, or association. This crabbed view of the original language ignores the vast body of material from both 1789 and the views of James Madison in the later years of his life.[16] As presented by Pike, if a majority wants to impose its own religious views on the community it does not have to establish an association; it merely takes existing civic institutions and makes them reflections of Christian theology. The church may not be established; religion, however, certainly is.

Sen. Robertson joined the discussion by stating, "As to the history of the official recognition of the fact that we are a Christian nation, it is crystal clear to me the bishop is right."[17] In one of the more ridiculous distortions of history, Robertson went on to remind his colleagues of Benjamin Franklin's call for prayer at the Constitutional Convention. Then he made the fraudulent assertion that Franklin "made a motion that every future session be opened with prayer, which was adopted, and they were opened with prayer." In fact, Franklin's motion, as previously noted, was never voted upon—it was conveniently ignored by Franklin's colleagues and it was never even brought to a vote. No session was ever opened with prayer. Of course, Robertson also insisted, "From the Bible we got our free enterprise system." This puts one in mind of the observation of his son, Pat, in 1981, that "the United States is only mentioned once in the Bible."[18]

Time was growing short and there were but two witnesses remaining. Rep. Frank Becker of New York, who was to be the champion of a constitutional amendment in the House two years hence, began his testimony, "While here I shall also advocate an amendment to the Constitution of the United States to permit prayer to Almighty God in public schools and all public places in the United States. On June 26, 1962, I introduced House Resolution 752, to amend the Constitution."[19]

Becker's amendment as first developed read as follows: "Section 1. Prayers may be offered in the course of any program in any public school or other public place in the United States." By quoting a sermon by Rabbi Bernard Zlotowitz of Long Island during his testimony,[20] Becker, made it clear that he was not asserting the nation was Christian, but Judeo-Christian. Becker agreed with the rabbi's displeasure that "today in our community and in some other communities, a group has seen fit to challenge this concept [the vital role of religion] of our American way of life and to undermine it."[21] We shall have ample opportunity to examine further Becker's views when we move to the House debates of 1964.

The final witness before the committee was Rep. John Dowdy of Texas. He noted, "I hope and trust, and, I dare to say, I pray that this honorable committee will take early action in the premises, that our children in our schools may again be permitted to voluntarily participate in uttering a prayer to our Creator."[22]

The committee adjourned and did not convene again on this subject for four years. It did allow numerous statements to be filed after the hearings closed, but in the two days of open discussion not a single supporter of the Supreme Court decision was heard. All ten witnesses and nine members of Congress recommended constitutional amendments.

By August the temper of the country was of such a character that Justice Tom Clark saw fit to clarify the Court's decision. He defended *Engel*, saying there was wide misunderstanding of the ruling. He criticized commentators who had interpreted the ruling as outlawing religious observances in the public schools. "In fact," he said, "it did nothing of the kind."[23]

Public Criticism

One of the earliest criticisms of the *Engel* ruling by a respected, mainstream Protestant scholar came from John Bennett, dean of Union Theological Seminary in New York. While prefacing his editorial in the August 6 issue of *Christianity and Crisis* with the caveat that the decision "may not in itself be objectionable," he feared that "the spirit of the opinions of the Court presage a negative attitude toward any such expression even if it is not written or prescribed by an agency of the state." Joining the fray on the side of what would later be defined as accommodationism, Bennett wrote:

> If the Court in the name of religious liberty tries to keep a lid on religious expression and teaching both in the public school and also in connection with experiments that involve cooperation with the public school, it will drive all religious communities to the establishment of parochial schools, much against the will of many, and to the great detriment of the public schools and probably of the quality of education.

In sum, Bennett called for "less absolutistic terms" of definition of church-state problems.[24]

As the fall approached with elections and the new school term, the pressure mounted for action against the Court decision. The Veterans of Foreign Wars meeting in Minneapolis called upon Congress to submit a constitutional amendment establishing the right to religious devotion "not only in the public schools of the nation, but also in all governmental agencies—national, state or local." The VFW castigated the Court and the delegates urged congressional passage of House Joint Resolution 752 which would permit school prayers.[25]

The editor of the Catholic journal *America* wrote an editorial in late August warning "our Jewish friends" that there have been "disturbing hints of heightened anti-Semitism" as a result of Jewish support for the Court's decision. The editor asked, "What will have been accomplished if our Jewish friends win all the legal immunities they seek" and bring upon themselves "social and cultural alienation?" Responding, the American Jewish Congress stated, "It is a sorry day for religious liberty in the United States when an effort to protect the guarantees of the First Amendment should evoke thinly veiled threats of anti-Semitism."[26]

The Protestant magazine *Christian Century* repeated the American Jewish Congress's language in its editorial on the subject.[27] Meanwhile the Catholic War Veterans went on record favoring a constitutional amendment authorizing daily prayer in all educational institutions, public and private. In late fall the American Legion joined in by urging Congress to enact legislation permitting "spoken" prayer in the nation's schools.[28]

In September the Religious News Service surveyed several states concerning school prayer and concluded, "first samplings of schools in 15 states indicates that they will continue their former practices of prayer and Bible reading without change." Most state officials interviewed drew a distinction between the New York State Board of Regents' prescribed prayer and the practice of Bible reading and reciting the Lord's Prayer.[29]

The most depressing news of the fall came when the House of Representatives voted unanimously to replace the stars on the wall above the speaker's desk with the motto "In God We Trust." In a speech before the House, Rep. Randall of Missouri opined that one of the "byproducts of our act today is that we have given perhaps not too directly, but in not too subtle a way, our answer to the recent decision of the U.S. Supreme Court

banning the Regents' Prayer from the New York public schools."
Speaker John McCormack said, "The words 'In God We Trust'
symbolize the path that our country has always taken since its
origin and pray God, will always take."[30] Meanwhile Richard
Nixon, temporarily out of work and running for governor of
California, weighed in favoring a constitutional amendment
legalizing the use of nonsectarian prayer in the public schools.

The House Convenes in Fall 1962

In the midst of this public uproar the Court assembled for the
fall and straight away agreed to hear appeals of two cases involving prayer and Bible reading in public schools in the states
of Pennsylvania and Maryland.

Meanwhile, Francis Cardinal Spellman joined the lists, proposing a constitutional amendment to correct a Supreme Court
"misreading of the no-establishment clause." A spokesman for
Spellman, filing the cardinal's views with the Senate Judiciary
Committee, noted that "our Constitution favors government cooperation with religion so long as such cooperation is devoid
of favored treatment to any one religion or denomination." It was
suggested to the committee that the Constitution be revised to
read: "Congress shall make no law respecting the establishment
of a state religion or, in encouraging religion, the preferment of
any religion or denomination, or prohibiting the free exercise of
religion." In justifying this language to the Senate, Cardinal Spellman's spokesman, Lawrence Cusack, noted that the American
people "can forever protect the no-establishment clause from the
doctrinaire absolutism of the secularists and restore a proper
balance between that clause and the free exercise of religion clause
of the First Amendment. . . . [It would] strike at the heart of

the doctrinaire and fallacious concept that there should be an absolute separation between Church and State."[31]

The *Schempp* Case, 1963

Nineteen sixty-three began quietly on the Supreme Court front. There were various resolutions on the subject of school prayer, including a strongly worded message to the Senate Judiciary Committee from deans and professors of forty-two law schools backing the Regents' prayer decision. They charged that the "intrusion of religion through devotional practices in the public school system both threatens the separation of Church and State and challenges the traditional integrity of the public schools."[32]

Briefly, the focus of Congress in relation to church-state issues seemed to be on federal aid to religious schools and more particularly aid to religious colleges. In addition, there was the continued challenge to Congress mounted by citizens who believed that federal aid to education should be paid in some form to parents so they might use the funds to select schools for their children. This early version of the current "choice" agenda was being promoted by a group called Citizens for Educational Freedom and candidates for Congress were being asked to take a position on the matter. But the interval between *Engel* and *Schempp* was brief indeed.

Oral arguments in *Schempp* took place on February 27 and 28, 1963. Many concerned persons on both sides of the issue seemed prepared to wait for that decision before further action. Interestingly, all the attorneys representing both sides in the two new cases affirmed agreement with *Engel,* because it was, for them, a clear case of a religious exercise required by government. No need was seen for a review of *Engel.* Justice Black's warning that a kind of local option might result from policies like that rejected in New York was taken to heart by many attorneys. They tended to agree with Justice Douglas that "the contest would be which church could get control of the school board."[33]

On June 17 the Court decided both *Schempp* and *Murray* by outlawing Bible reading in public schools. In his opinion Justice Tom Clark extended the *Engel* decision by establishing purpose and effect tests regarding establishment. For a law to be valid, "there must be a secular legislative purpose and a primary effect that neither advances nor inhibits religion."[34] Most leaders of mainline Protestant churches applauded the decision. Episcopal Bishop Gerald Burrill of Chicago commended the ruling saying it "dissipates the myth that ours is a Christian country. . . . [It] should clear the air and put the challenge squarely up to the churches and Christian parents." Contrary opinion was offered by Billy Graham, who said he was "shocked," and that the Court was "wrong. . . . At a time when moral decadence is evident on every hand, when race tension is mounting, when the threat of communism is growing, when terrifying new weapons of destruction are being created, we need more religion, not less." He called the decision a penalty for the 80 percent of Americans who "want Bible reading and prayer in the schools."

Cardinal Spellman deplored the decision. "I think it will do great harm to our country and there is nothing we can do but bear it. But nevertheless, no one who believes in God . . . can approve such a decision." Cardinals Cushing and McIntyre had earlier attacked the decision. Archbishop Robert Lucey stated, "Now that God has been banished from our public schools, I fear that the Declaration of Independence is in jeopardy."[35] In the South Gov. George Wallace said Alabama would defy the Court's stand. "I don't care what they say in Washington, we are going to keep right on praying and reading the Bible in the public schools of Alabama." No doubt such practices had provided Wallace with his high sense of morality respecting race relations. Gov. Ross Barnett of Mississippi planned to advise teachers to ignore the Supreme Court. In contrast with southern political leaders, there appeared to be a mood of compliance among their counterparts in the North.[36]

By mid-July Rep. Frank Becker of New York had introduced a resolution to amend the Constitution and within a day he had twenty-two signatures on a discharge petition. The mood was such that the Religious News Service offered the opinion, "Congress will take action before fall to submit such an amendment to the states for ratification."[37] By September Becker had convinced sixty colleagues, many of whom had introduced amendments themselves, to join in a single effort. Becker was seeking 218 signatures on a discharge petition to force the bill, House Joint Resolution 9, out of committee. The wording would amend the Constitution with three sections.

Section 1. Nothing in this Constitution shall be deemed to prohibit the offering, reading from, or listening to prayers or Biblical Scriptures, if participation therein is on a voluntary basis, in any government or public school, institution, or public place.

Section 2. Nothing in this Constitution shall be deemed to prohibit making reference to belief in, reliance upon, or invoking the aid of God or a Supreme Being, in any governmental or public document, proceeding, activity, ceremony, school, institution, or place upon any coinage, currency, or obligation of the United States.

Section 3. Nothing in this Article shall constitute an establishment of religion.

Two criticisms of the Court in late August are noteworthy. The Vatican publication *Osservatore Romano* referred to the Court decision, suggesting that the principle of church-state separation in the United States "is tending to become, also legally agnosticism."[38] Actually, this critique may be the most perceptive, although coming from a source that opposed *Engel.* In fact, it may be argued that the Court was confirming that the state is agnostic, taking no position on the accuracy of religious claims of whatever character or nature.

In Los Angeles Billy Graham spoke to a crusade audience at the Memorial Coliseum. He decried the "trend to take God and moral law out of our schools," warning that the society is entering the "age of the shrug." He said separation "was never meant to separate school children from God. . . . The trend of taking God and moral teaching from the schools is a diabolical scheme and it is bearing its fruit in the deluge of juvenile delinquency which is overwhelming our nation."[39] The stage was set for a major confrontation when Congress convened again in 1964.

Notes

1. Religious News Service, *Religious Herald,* May 17, 1962, p. 3.
2. Ibid., October 4, 1962, p. 3.
3. Ibid., August 16, 1962, p. 3.
4. *New York Times,* June 26, 1962.
5. Ibid., June 27, 1962.
6. Ibid., June 28, 1962.
7. Ibid., July 1, 1962.
8. Religious News Service, *Religious Herald,* July 26, 1962, p. 3.
9. U.S. Congress, Senate, Hearings Before the Committee on the

Judiciary, *Prayers in Public Schools and Other Matters* (Washington, D.C.: U.S. Government Printing Office, 1963).

10. Ibid., p. 28.

11. Ibid., p. 43.

12. Ibid., p. 47.

13. Ibid., p. 2.

14. Ibid., p. 51.

15. Ibid., p. 55.

16. See particularly Jasper Adams letter.

17. U.S. Congress, Senate Hearings, *Prayers in Public Schools,* p. 68.

18. "700 Club" broadcast, 1981, tape.

19. U.S. Congress, Senate Hearings, *Prayers in Public Schools,* p. 70.

20. Through a serious error in the editing of the Senate Hearings for 1962, the impression was left that Rep. Becker was Jewish. In fact, he was Roman Catholic. The confusion was the result of attributing to Becker about two pages of material written by Rabbi Zlotowitz.

21. U.S. Congress, Senate Hearings, *Prayers in Public Schools,* p. 73.

22. Ibid., p. 81.

23. Religious News Service, *Religious Herald,* August 23, 1962, p. 3.

24. Ibid., p. 20.

25. Religious News Service, *Religious Herald,* August 30, 1962, p. 3.

26. *New York Times,* August 27, 1962.

27. Religious News Service, *Religious Herald,* September 13, 1962, p. 20.

28. Ibid., November 1, 1962, p. 3.

29. Ibid., September 20, 1962, p. 3.

30. Ibid., October 18, 1962, p. 3.

31. Ibid., November 1, 1962, p. 21.

32. Ibid., January 3, 1963, p. 20.

33. Ibid., March 14, 1963, p. 14.

34. Contained in that decision were the roots of the later, three-part "Lemon test" advanced by Justice Warren Burger in the 1971 *Lemon v. Kurtzman* decision.

35. Religious News Service, *Religious Herald,* July 4, 1963, pp. 3, 10.

36. Ibid., July 11, 1963, p. 3.

37. Ibid., July 25, 1963, p. 3.

38. Ibid., August 29, 1963, p. 21.

39. Ibid., September 5, 1963, p. 3. Leo Pfeffer, chief legal counsel for the American Jewish Congress, was a primary player in the successful arguments before the Court in the *Engel* and *Schempp* cases. Those victories were the fruits of a ten-year period of strategy seeking to find the best vehicle to challenge Bible reading and prayer. In the aftermath of the *McCollum* decision of 1948 there had been a sharp criticism leveled by Catholics and Protestants against the loss of what they saw as a Christian privilege. In Pfeffer's mind it was not the time to challenge prayer and Bible reading in public schools. But there was a case before the Court, *Doremus*, that addressed those issues. While he entered reluctantly into an amicus brief in that case, Pfeffer "was pessimistic that the Court would allow the Bible reading statute [New Jersey] to stand and feared the negative consequences of such a decision" in the public arena. He wished to build, at a future time, a careful, well-argued case that would lay out the First Amendment principles on which to reject public school Bible reading and prayer. He did not view *Doremus* as that opportunity. Pfeffer was relieved when the case was dismissed on procedural grounds in 1952. (See the excellent forthcoming volume by Gregg Ivers, *To Build a Wall: American Jews and the Separation of Church and State.*)

With the advange of forty years of history, it is evident that Pfeffer was correct. Our appraisal of the fifties and the presidential outlook of both Truman and Eisenhower suggests that, even compared with the events of 1962 and following, a more vitriolic response to a Court ruling against prayer or Bible reading would likely have occurred in 1952. In addition, by 1962 the coalition formed between Catholic and Protestant leaders in response to *McCollum* had disappeared and mainline Protestant leaders, led by Dean Kelley, supported *Engel* and *Schempp*, as of course did President Kennedy.

8

House and Senate Hearings, 1964-66

The 1964 House Hearings

Early in 1964, after much delay and accusations from many colleagues that he was bottling up the issue, word from Washington came that Rep. Emanuel Celler, chairman of the House Judiciary Committee, was prepared to go forward with hearings on Bible reading and prayer in public schools sometime during the year. Prior to that decision Celler had directed his staff to do an exhaustive examination of the issues raised by the constitutional amendments, including the Becker version. True to their mandate they developed an extended background study that warned of countless legal thickets for any amendment. More important, the inquiry found there were more than eighteen thousand religious bodies in the country that had fewer than fifty thousand members. The total for all of them was about two million, in sharp contrast with the relatively small number of religious groups with more than fifty thousand adherents, a figure regularly employed by amendment proponents to suggest how easily such amendments might be implemented.

The amendment (House Joint Resolution 693) introduced in 1962 into a Senate hearing by Rep. Frank Becker was the focus in 1964 for a discharge petition that early in the year had amassed 125 of the necessary 218 signatures to take the matter out of the House Judiciary Committee's hands. In February the House Republican Policy Committee endorsed a constitutional amendment similar to that offered by Rep. Becker. Finally, late in March Rep. Celler announced hearings that would begin on April 22. Becker had by that time increased the number of signatures for discharge to 161.

Even as he announced plans for the committee, Celler positioned himself against the avalanche of prayer resolutions, numbering 144, that were on the table for consideration. He asked, "Whose prayer will it be? Who will determine the prayer—the state, county, school board, parish . . . or the precinct level? If it's done locally, will not the majority denomination determine the prayer?" Meanwhile Becker, representing Long Island, accused Celler of intentionally scheduling his appearance on the opening day of the New York World's Fair.

As April 22 approached Georgia Gov. Carl Sanders and the mayor of Atlanta joined several Atlanta Protestant ministers to proclaim "Return the Bible to Our Schools Day."[1] It seemed to amendment supporters like a sign predicting success. Resolutions from the U.S. Junior Chamber of Commerce and Project Prayer, a group led by actors Victor Jory, Dale Evans, Roy Rogers, Lloyd Nolan, Colleen Gray, and Gene Autry, were evidence of strong support across the country. Less visible, but ultimately more significant, was a gathering in New York in March, led by Dean Kelley of the National Council of Churches, who began a major campaign to enlist religious leaders and lawyers against the Becker proposal.

Observers present for the first session of the hearings held April 22 noted a considerable tension as Chairman Celler gavelled the committee into session.[2]

The first witness was Frank Becker. He quickly inserted the barb that he had been urging such hearings for twenty-two months. He noted, "The welfare and the entire future of our beloved America depends upon how we handle the most dynamic tradition in our national life—dependence upon Almighty God."[3] Almost immediately Becker came to verbal blows with the committee counsel, who challenged Becker's use of a sermon by New York Rabbi Bernard Zlotowitz, pointing out that the sermon was delivered before the *Engel* decision and that the rabbi had sent a letter to Becker stating, "I have grave doubts on the efficacy of a constitutional amendment. I am truly sorry to disappoint you. I trust you will understand."[4] A similar contradiction was in store for Becker when he read from a 1922 statement by Catholic Cardinal Gibbons. Becker claimed it proved the respected cleric favored Bible reading in public schools. Committee counsel produced a letter by Gibbons specifically disapproving that practice.

Although he was embarrassed by his documentary default, Becker pressed on. Quickly sparks flew between him and Chairman Celler, with supporters of each weighing in with advice about procedure. Becker, becoming agitated, as were many of his colleagues, accused atheists who opposed his bill of being unpatriotic. As he continued his remarks Becker quoted extensively, from prominent religious figures from around the country. Billy Graham was cited and quoted as saying, "We have reaped a whirlwind in delinquency. Young people do not know what is right or wrong any more. Our young people are not being taught moral values; they are at sea morally. . . . I back the Becker amendment."[5] Playing the other side of the Christian street, Becker quoted from Cardinal Spellman, who claimed the Supreme Court decision was "out of line with the conscience and religious heritage of the American people and one which foreshadows an ominous tendency to undermine cherished tradition of this nation."

Becker thrust into the debate the argument that excision of mandated prayers in the schools violated the free exercise of those who wanted it. He was quite prepared to accept the proposition that the prayers should be nondenominational. He was asked by Rep. Carleton King of New York "We don't have any denominational prayer in the House, Senate, or in our courts, do we, Mr. Becker?" Becker replied, "None that I know."[6]

An examination of the prayers offered in the House and Senate on that very day reveal a great deal about the understanding of "nondenominational prayer" by Becker and his supporters. The chaplain, Bernard Braskamp, opened the House that day with a prayer that had as its text Revelation 2:10 and closed with the words, "In Christ's name we pray. Amen." That was the normal complementary close for Braskamp's prayers. Nondenominational? Perhaps, for Christians, but Becker argued throughout his presentation that Jews were to have their faith respected. A similar prayer came from the lips of the Senate chaplain that day, Frederick Brown Harris, who closed with his usual phrase, "We ask it in the Redeemer's name. Amen." Some days he became more particular, ending with "In the name of Christ Jesus, our Lord, we ask it."[7]

As the debate progressed in the committee most of the arguments that would be repeated for decades to come emerged. Frequent reference was made to the term "voluntary," with definitions at a minimum. Usually the word applied to a school's right to choose and the pupil's right to respond to the school mandate. Reflecting the Zorach decision, a minority advocated a principle of released time for prayer.

When the committee reconvened after lunch it was reported that Becker was ill and could not return. It could have been his way of getting back at Celler for the scheduling of the hearing on the World Fair's opening day. In any event, Becker returned to face the committee again on the fourth day.

Becker's return brought forth extended, sometimes heated, exchanges filling over forty pages in the committee record. The most clearly combative questioning came from Celler and Rep. James Corman of California. Little was resolved in the time expended. Again efforts were made to have Becker define what he meant by "nondenominational" or "nonsectarian." He was asked where could one get such a prayer. Along the same line, Becker was questioned as to whether the Bible was sectarian. In particular, what was to be made of the fact that Catholics and Protestants did not agree on the proper translation of the Bible? A final point, left quite vague, was the degree to which any prayer authorized by the Becker amendment might be prescribed and by whom. Impatient, acid remarks frequently dotted the dialogue.

Orchestrating the hearings to provide maximum exposure to those opposed to prayer amendments, Celler opened the first afternoon session with some twenty documents he had received. Thirteen of the letters or statements opposed amendments, seven favored. Notable among the opponents were the United Presbyterian Church General Assembly, Bishop John Wesley Lord, the *Washington Post*, Harvard law professor Erwin Griswold, and theologian Reinhold Niebuhr, who wrote:

> I do not think it would be wise to enshrine a detailed method of preserving religious rites in the public schools. We are the most pluralistic society in the world. The separation of church and state, ordained in the Constitution, is the only general method of doing justice to all aspects of this pluralism. I should

hope that various cities and States would experiment with religious practices which do not violate the Constitution. But it would be a mistake to enshrine any of these ad hoc adjustments to our religious heterogeneity into the Constitution.[8]

Griswold's comments became an oft-revisited point of contention. Proponents of the amendments rightly pointed to the professor's objections to the Court entering the field of school prayer. One of the few respected constitutional authorities to so state the case, he was a natural ally for Becker advocates. Unfortunately for them, Griswold still came down against any amendments, as was regularly recalled by amendment opponents when his name was employed.

Two Republicans on the committee, William Cahill of New Jersey and John Lindsay of New York, early raised serious objections to the tone of the debate. Lindsay urged that people supporting an amendment not imply that those questioning it were "somehow anti-God in the process, or antimorality, or anti-children, antimotherhood." He was joined by Cahill, who commented:

I would hope that the witnesses, if I may specify, rather than generalize, would answer specifically three questions as they testify. . . . Who will authorize what prayer, and what Bible? . . . How can we get a prayer that is tolerable to all creeds and preferential to none, and who is going to be the ultimate determining judge as to what prayer is to be used, what version of the Bible is to be used?[9]

As that first afternoon wore on a parade of congressional members appeared to endorse amendments they had proposed. One must assume that since a majority of the 144 amendments offered were similar to the Becker version, there was a modicum of posturing for local consumption on the part of many of the legislators.

One of the more interesting exchanges came between Rep. J. Edgar Chenoweth of Colorado and committee member George Senner of Arizona. Chenoweth had proposed an amendment that would, he said, not constitute an establishment of religion. Senner responded, "What this resolution does, in my opinion, is establish a new religion. You break down the old ones."[10] Chenoweth disagreed, but Senner persisted. "But any time that we pray to God we are practicing a religious ritual."

The question of defining "nonsectarian" religion and "voluntary" quickly became an area of contention. In the afternoon Rep. King insisted, "The Bible is not a sectarian book and the Lord's Prayer is not a sectarian prayer. . . . The Lord's Prayer is a statement of personal inadequacy, a petition for the forgiveness of sins and a plea for guidance in our daily lives."[11]

The exchange between Chenoweth and Senner, and ultimately involving Rep. Don Edwards of California, encapsulated much of the conflict over these issues, which would continue unabated for nearly thirty years.

SENNER: The point I am trying to make is this: Aren't we establishing a religion when we let a school board determine what the children either must participate in involuntarily or be excused from and be criticized by their fellow students for leaving the room?

CHENOWETH: I will say to my good friend I think it is largely a matter of semantics. I have briefed this question on just what the word "religion" implies. I think to some degree we are a religious nation. We are certainly not an atheistic nation. We condemn the Communists because they don't believe in God, but in the United States we boast of our belief in God.

SENNER: I agree with my colleague. I have two boys and they are attending Virginia schools. We are Lutherans. There is nothing in the Supreme Court decision that would prevent my boys from taking their pocket Bibles to school and reading during free hours. Isn't that true?

CHENOWETH: That is right.

SENNER: There is nothing that prevents them from praying at any time they want to in our schools now.

CHENOWETH: That is right.

SENNER: But many of the general public believe this is prohibited by the decision of the Supreme Court.

CHENOWETH: Not any private devotion. I never heard that question raised before. It is the classroom prayer and reading of the Scripture which is objected to by certain individuals for reasons of their own.

SENNER: Under the present Supreme Court decisions, isn't it true that my children, whether in Wisconsin, Mississippi, Arizona, or Virginia, can pray any time they want to or read from their own Bible?

CHENOWETH: Just the same as you and I have the same right. We can do the same thing.

SENNER: We can do it in the school during our free periods.

CHENOWETH: Yes, anywhere. I want to make sure we preserve that privilege.

SENNER: I hope we never lose it.

CHENOWETH: I agree with you.

EDWARDS: Judge, you are asking the State governments to make up prayers?

CHENOWETH: No, I don't want any government agency composing these prayers.

EDWARDS: Or a subdivision thereof?

CHENOWETH: No; no school board or any similar group.

EDWARDS: You do not suggest that any subdivision of the State should have the power to make up a prayer?

CHENOWETH: No, not in the least. I am not suggesting that. I am sorry if I said anything which may have left that impression. The Supreme Court went into this matter in the New York case. It said the board of regents has no such authority. Maybe they are right on that point.

EDWARDS: In other words, the board of regents should not have the power?

CHENOWETH: No, not in the least. I think the substance of the prayer and form of the prayer—

EDWARDS: Who do you think ought to make up the prayer?

CHENOWETH: The teacher in the classroom as well as anyone. There should be no difficulty in agreeing on the form of a similar prayer.

EDWARDS: Is that not government?

CHENOWETH: You can draw your own inferences. As a boy I participated in this exercise and I never heard these questions raised or anyone criticized on the form of the prayer.

EDWARDS: Do you believe that the local school boards should be able to compose a prayer?

CHENOWETH: No, I would not give this authority to the school boards. I don't believe the school boards in Colorado ever composed a prayer. I never heard of it being done. The New York regents composed a prayer which the Supreme Court objected to. It was a New York case. I don't know that this situation exists in any other State.

EDWARDS: Who is supposed to make up the prayer that is contemplated in your resolution?

CHENOWETH: You mean the prayer that is offered?

EDWARDS: Yes.

CHENOWETH: The Lord's Prayer can be offered, or the teacher can compose a simple prayer. I think the board of regents did a pretty good job in writing the prayer for the New York schools. I didn't see anything wrong in it. But there is objection to the school board or the regents preparing the prayer. I am not in favor of giving them this authority. Let the teachers write the prayers, or perhaps the students. They could suggest as good a prayer as anyone else. I didn't mean to infer that the board should have this authority.[12]

This engagement over the issues was a fair exchange. It helped to clarify the meaning of the term "voluntary" as frequently employed in the debate. It was agreed by all that voluntary when applied to students was unrestricted by Court decisions. If "voluntary" were used to describe a prohibition by the Court it must, then, apply to schools voluntarily establishing prayers that students could voluntarily avoid. Senner felt that such a structure constituted establishing religion. Chenoweth saw it otherwise and insisted he would not favor government authorship of prayers. Pressed by Edwards, he agreed that the teacher could compose the prayer. But was not the teacher acting as a government agent?

Here the exchange broke down. As we shall discover, the Justice Department in its argument on *Lee* v. *Weisman* in 1992 agreed that classroom prayer was necessarily coercive because it was administered by a school official. It was that position that ultimately closed the book on a thirty-year debate.

One other significant point was established when Chenoweth spoke of a "good job in writing the prayer" and noted that students could "suggest as good a prayer as anyone else." The question to be posed at that point is obvious. Who will define what is a "good" prayer? Chenoweth's position was quite typical and reflected a culturally conditioned notion that prayer was definable within Christian parameters. Indeed, this predisposition to confine religious definitions to majority views led to the establishment of the term "Judeo-Christian tradition," an unfortunate if well-intended hyphenate. Jews do not have a Christian heritage, while Christians most certainly do have a Jewish heritage. Therefore, Jewish citizens do not, in point of fact, have a Judeo-Christian tradition. It is an effort at tolerance that is flawed by an inherent imbalance.

The first day of the hearings ended, as they had begun, with a plea for amending the Constitution. Rep. John Anderson of Illinois insisted, "Do not destroy the rights of the majority, I beg you, merely to placate the minority by placing an unwarranted interpretation on the intent, purpose, or scope of this proposed amendment." Anderson encapsulated in his remarks the precise difficulty James Madison saw in democratic majorities.

As the eighteen days of hearings passed, from April 22 to June 3, a pattern developed. There were numerous insertions into the record of correspondence directed to the chairman and other committee members. Dozens of representatives were heard from, most briefly, pushing their versions of an amendment. The focus seemed always to return to the Becker option. Hundreds of individuals and groups were heard from in those long days. Some of the testimony bears repeating either because of personalities or historical significance. For the reader with an insatiable appetite for such material, the three-volume *School Prayers* publication by the committee, running to 2,774 pages, is seldom checked out of repositories that possess it.

The second day of hearings was filled with prepared testimony from the dozens of congressmen who had submitted prayer amendments. The chair opened the day by inserting into the record several statements by religious groups and leaders—Episcopalians, Presbyterians, Jews, Baptists. Then came once more the barrage of support for some kind of amendment. Rep. Louis Wyman of New Hampshire reasoned that children should be exposed to the "concept of the Supreme Being whether or not the concept is rational or logical, because this helps to develop in the child a conscience to keep him, for example, from being a Communist or a nonbeliever."[13] Further, he insisted that if a prayer amendment were passed it would override all those clauses in state constitutions that forbade such prayers. Wyman's position on federal imposition of prayer rulings moved into the home itself.

> To leave prayer exercises solely in the home or in the church is to mean that for many children there will be no prayers at all and no exposure to prayer, for, unfortunately, too many parents are too busy, too disinterested, or outright disinclined. It is important in this world that we in the United States should be on God's side.[14]

As the day drew to a close Chairman Celler had this rather interesting exchange with Rep. D. R. Matthews of Florida. Celler asked if Florida had always had prayer in public schools. "As far as I can remember, Mr. Chairman, yes," he responded. Celler asked, "Would you say that the morals of the young people are better in your State than in a State that doesn't allow Bible reading or prayers in the school?" Matthews answered, "Yes, I think they are."[15]

On the third day Celler once again inserted into the record a large number of documents from persons and organizations opposed to amendments. Of the nearly score of statements only two favored amending the Constitution. Strong opposition was voiced by the American Jewish Congress and the Orthodox Jewish Congress. As the direct testimony resumed Rep. Joe Waggonner of Louisiana made an extended justification for an amendment. With obvious passion he insisted:

> We cannot even hope to win the cold war unless we are totally conscious that there is a God, that He has endowed us with inalienable rights, and that even the state is subject to His law. To hang around the neck of proud Americans this albatross of agnostic orthodoxy which the Supreme Court has done, and to associate the Government of the United States with it, is to repudiate the Declaration of Independence and the statement that we are endowed by our Creator with certain inalienable rights.[16]

Representative B. F. Sisk of California took a contrary view in one of the few statements by a congressman who came before the Committee opposed to an amendment. He insisted:

> One of the basic reasons why I am so vigorous in my opposition to the resolution is that what it is proposed that we do, as I would interpret it, is to have religion by majority rule. In other words, by popular choice. . . . The minority in the community must be protected against political majorities.[17]

The fifth day brought a major shift in the tone of the testimony. A series of advocates against an amendment generated extensive conversation among committee members. Edwin H. Tuller was the first spokesperson for the National Council of Churches. Quoting from NCC board action he noted, "We recognize the wisdom as well as the authority of this ruling [Engel]. But whether prayers may be offered at special occasions in the public schools may well be left to the judgment of the board responsible for the program of the public schools in the local community."[18]

Tuller, in language that anticipated the arguments of the government on behalf of the school in Lee v. Weisman, went on to explain. "The last sentence quoted is designed to distinguish between required daily prayers in classrooms, which are not countenanced, and prayers at commencements or special assemblies, which may be if the local board desires." Expanding later on this theme Tuller stated, "There is no doubt but what our Nation is a nation under God, and we have no objection to recognizing it as such. It is the compulsory part of stating that the day shall begin with a prayer." Rep. William Cahill of New Jersey challenged him on this distinction. "But what I find it very difficult to do in my own mind is to understand your objection on that basis and understand your willingness to have these prayers said at special assemblies in the same school."[19]

Tuller continued to focus on his primary theme with several points. (1) It is not right for the majority to impose religious beliefs or practices on the minority in public institutions. (2) Public schools are particularly inappropriate places for corporate religious exercises. (3) Children are almost always not given a genuinely free choice by glib use of the word "voluntary participation," when the whole atmosphere of the classroom is one of compliance and conformity to group activities. (4) Who is to compose the prayers, and who is to select the Scriptures? (5)

What a nonsectarian theistic majority can require today in the way of a regents prayer or Bible reading "without comment" a sectarian majority can require tomorrow in the way of an Augsburg Confession, a Hail Mary, or a theistic tract. (6) Religious practices that are nonsectarian are too vague and generalized to have much meaning or effect for character development or moral motivation, whereas practices that are specific or demanding enough to effect character or motivation are unacceptable to some and therefore sectarian.[20]

Tuller insisted, "I live in fear of identifying this [the regents' prayer] with prayer. Because if the children are taught this prayer, then my teaching that prayer is a vital relationship between the individual and his Creator through Jesus Christ is contrary to that teaching. This is my fear, sir."[21]

The next witness, Charles Tuttle, general counsel for the National Council of Churches, provided a wide-ranging discussion of the term voluntary as he sought to clarify how that word should be understood in light of the Supreme Court opinions. He stated in a colloquy with Chairman Celler:

I find nothing in the U.S. Constitution and nothing in these decisions that prevents a human being with a religious conscience, whether he is old or young, from undertaking to pray. I find nothing in the Supreme Court which in any way does anything but encourage that. . . .

I think what the Court was referring to was whether the organization of a prayer by State authority and presenting it in school as a religious exercise to be part of the educational program among children who are compelled to attend that school by operation of law, that kind of a prayer, the arm of the State reaching into religion, was not less objectionable because some child might wish to remain silent.[22]

On the morning of April 30 the chairman introduced Bishop Fulton Sheen, the religious star of network television in the 1950s. Sheen declared that a constitutional amendment was required because (1) the Supreme Court's decision was founded on a myth that there was a danger of a union between church and state; (2) the Court took lawmaking out of the hands of the legislature; (3) the Court decision exceeded the competency of any human court. In short order the bishop directed the committee to his favorite subject—communism. "If we allow a court to say, 'No. There shall be the freedom not to pray,' without affirming the freedom to pray; a minority group will succeed in lawmaking through the Supreme Court and write into our Constitution the next conclusion; namely, article 124 of the Soviet Constitution." While Sheen was disarmingly congenial to a minimum prayer— "In god we trust"—in the schools, under questioning he saw a maximum allowable activity as well. He supported Bible reading in the classroom. His point was best conveyed as he closed his testimony by commenting on the role of the Supreme Court. "They may only reaffirm the freedom to pray and the freedom not to pray."[23]

Alabama Gov. George Wallace also testified in the afternoon, bringing his special brand of states rights dogma to the committee. He had several spirited exchanges with members who were of other minds on that subject. He shed no new light on the discussion of the Becker amendment.

Another witness for the afternoon was attorney Leo Pfeffer of New York. He was a firm advocate of church/state separation and testified vigorously against amendments. At one point he spoke of the completely erroneous assumption advanced by Wallace and Sheen that "the Supreme Court or any decision of the Supreme Court or any courts of the United States from the lowest to the highest courts have forbidden children to read the

Bible or pray in public schools. Nothing could be further from the truth." The Court said, "The State through its agencies cannot promote or establish the reading of the Bible or recitation of prayers. Nothing at all to the effect that the children may not . . . pray in the public school."[24]

As the hearing moved into May the surprises were all but over. Predictable remarks by legislators continued unabated. Significantly, no witness was forthcoming from the White House. This was a House of Representatives show, unlike the orchestrated Senate hearings of the 1980s which bore the unmistakable imprint of the Reagan/Bush administration. It is also worthy of notice that in 1964 there was no voice in the political arena for millions of fundamentalists. Billy Graham was quoted but did not testify. The National Association of Evangelicals claimed two million members, but that organization represented existing denominations, not huge individual churches with thousands of members. It did see itself as "servicing" some ten million more through various affiliates. And, indeed, the NAE did testify in favor of a constitutional amendment. But the rhetoric was muted, civil, and brief. Most Americans were only vaguely aware of what was to become the core of the Moral Majority. In the 1960s extreme fundamentalism was at most apolitical. Television was not an option for most of them in 1964. To be sure Jerry Falwell and Rex Humbard had syndicated weekly shows, but they were seldom viewed by other than the converted. Pat Robertson did not go on the air until 1965.[25]

One of the most productive exchanges came on May 8, when the committee heard from professor of church history Franklin Littell of Chicago Theological Seminary. His was one of the most cogent and thoughtful analyses offered during the hearings. Addressing the distinction between toleration and freedom, Littell remarked on Madison's use of natural rights:

The reference to natural rights is important, for it shows the context of religious liberty. That liberty, they declared, was neither created nor granted by government: It was "prior" (logically not chronologically) to the frame of government itself. Much of the present discussion is wrongly conceived and wrongly directed, for it presupposes a history of toleration rather than an affirmation of liberty. In fact the whole discussion of religious liberty ends as wrong as it begins if the political question is primary; that is, "What are the political benefits to be derived from efficient use of religion?" Most of the so-called prayer amendments are set within the context of toleration rather than liberty, as the repetition of the demurrer reveals: "Nothing in this article shall constitute an establishment of religion." The same misapprehension would seem to lie back of the apology for arrangements in the prayer cases, which generously provide that dissenters may remain silent or be excused from the room. This is not the atmosphere of liberty, but rather the style of toleration.[26]

On May 14 the committee had its largest attendance, thirty-one of the thirty-five members present to hear testimony from actor Victor Jory and actress Colleen Gray. They represented Project Prayer. While there was a mild threat to muster support through television if the committee failed to report the amendment to the floor, the drama lay in the personalities, not the content.

Following the actors came the American Civil Liberties Union, represented by Edward Miller and Lawrence Speiser. It was a civilized discussion between the two men and a number of skeptics on the committee. Of particular interest was Miller's commentary on the teacher as prayer director. "I say that no public school board has a right to inquire into the religious affiliation of the teacher in choosing her, or whether she believes in any religion. . . . Therefore, I don't think a public school teacher is the one to read the prayer or Bible."[27] Of course, Miller didn't believe anyone ought to perform that function, but the point was made that unless you knew the teacher's religion you would not know whether he or she was prepared to carry out the task.

The next to last testimony of May 15 came from Martin Marty, a professor at the University of Chicago Divinity School. Demonstrating both the class and intellect that have distinguished him for some thirty years since, Marty opposed Becker and argued:

> You cannot teach the history of the West, or Hawthorne, Melville, Abraham Lincoln, the Founding Fathers, to even a first, second, third, and fourth grader without confronting religion. In teaching a much more free and open situation is had than in devotion. I am trying to express a sympathy with those who have a genuine concern for the future of American religion. But, I feel they are thoroughly mistaken in the recourse they are taking. Meanwhile, the First Amendment will protect all minorities from the religion of "ruling elites" or unofficial establishments, from governmental gods and religions, from the tyranny of local religious majorities and will guarantee "free exercise" of religion in the persuasive institutions we now enjoy.[28]

The final days of the hearings produced few new ideas. Rep. Becker reappeared on May 20 to present written testimony from Rabbi Jonas Simon. As he read the rabbi's words about the Supreme Court reversing U.S. spiritual heritage while encouraging modernism and communism, Chairman Celler was clearly agitated. In his final exchange with Becker Celler exploded:

> CELLER: Mr. Becker, I have listened to this jeremiad; I can't think of anything else to call it, but jeremiad. I must also make comment that this good rabbi, and I assume that he is a good

rabbi, is guilty of complete distortion of facts in his statement. He misreads the Supreme Court decisions. He gives disjointed conclusions from imaginary premises. He misreads history and he sums up imaginary ills and evil practices, wholly unrelated to the Supreme Court decision and to the question at hand; namely, whether we should or should not adopt the constitutional amendment. Finally, I would say with all due respect to the good rabbi, that the whole statement is a lot of sound and fury signifying nothing.

BECKER: I assumed, Mr. Chairman, you would reach such conclusions, being opposed to any action at all.

CELLER: It is not a question of being opposed to it, but I am opposed to the fulminations of this man of the cloth who makes such irresponsible statements and the entire statement is a tissue of irresponsible assertions.

BECKER: I might respectfully disagree with the chairman of the committee because I have a high regard for this man and his talents and his learning and the things he has tried to promote for the good of mankind and the salvation of this country.[29]

The committee took a week off and, quite by accident, conventions representing perhaps twenty million Baptists held a massive meeting in New Jersey.

The Case of Billy Graham

In the spring of 1964 the Becker Amendment was in the news daily. We have examined the seven weeks of hearings before the House of Representatives Committee on the Judiciary. The prominent missing witness, as noted above, was Billy Graham, a chief advocate of the Becker approach from the beginning. He was one of the earliest challengers of the Supreme Court in 1962, eager to advance the cause of prayer. Yet Graham declined to appear before the House committee and confined his remarks to press conferences, speaking engagements, and crusades. He made clear his support of the Becker amendment at the Southern Baptist Convention in May 1964. He played on the word non-sectarian, as had many committee witnesses. If only one could devise a nonsectarian prayer, it was argued, then mandating such in the schools would be appropriate. While there was debate over whether the regents' prayer was of such a nature, Graham asserted that if it were not, a mere tinkering with the wording could make it so. Lurking in the background was the question about the Lord's Prayer, a clearly sectarian alternative.

Baptists from all across the nation assembled in Atlantic City that spring to celebrate 150 years of organized activity in the United States. The Triennial Convention of Baptists had been established in 1814. Since the Civil War era the unity had been fractured several times, but bravely American Baptists, Southern Baptists, the National Baptist Convention, U.S.A., the National Baptist Convention of America, and a number of smaller unions gathered to celebrate a long lost vision. For Southern Baptists it was a time to show off their muscle in the midst of "lesser groups." Naturally, Billy Graham was there, speaking and making numerous pronouncements to the press. On May 24, 1964, Graham held a press conference in conjunction with his address to the convention. In a large press room just off the main arena Graham was in his element, confronting a generally congenial religious press. Standing behind a table, Graham carefully positioned his "red rubber Bible" in front of him as he fielded questions to which, always, the Bible had the answer. I led him into a discussion of the Becker amendment. With notable enthusiasm he offered his personal support for a constitutional amendment that would allow Bible reading and organized prayer in the public schools. He waxed eloquent about the need for moral influence in our schools. He saw a catalyst for such moral influence in what he termed "nonsectarian" prayer and praise.

At the time I was reporting for a Virginia journal.[30] I posed a question: Did Graham believe that only through the "God in Christ" could one be assured of eternal salvation? Reacting to the question eagerly and with Bible now in hand, Graham warmed to what he must surely have sensed was a supportive inquiry. He certainly did believe that, he affirmed. A second question: Did Graham think that Jews had to believe in God as defined in the Christian faith in order to obtain that salvation? His ardor only slightly cooled, Graham affirmed that such was the case. Then the third question: "How then can you speak of nonsectarian prayer when you affirm there is only one God and that deity can only be known in Jesus Christ? What God, as you define God, would be equally acceptable to Jew and Christian alike?" Flustered, Graham responded with a question: "Do you mean the God up there or the God in Christ?" Asked if that meant there were two gods, in an aggravated state he then dismissed the questioner as lacking in proper knowledge of Christian history.

The problem here is clear. Graham wanted to insist upon the United States being a Christian nation, a concept that automatically creates second-class citizenship for non-Christians.[31] Yet he had enough understanding of democracy to detect a problem in the schools if Christianity were actively promoted. Nonsectarian prayer was the buzz word applied to avoid offense.

The term "nonsectarian" is extremely difficult to define in its modern use. For decades it has been applied to prayers at public occasions or in public schools. Removing the formula "In

Jesus' name we pray" from an otherwise generic Jewish/Christian prayer was thought to cleanse the prayer of sectarian bias. Of course it doesn't; it only makes it slightly more inclusive for people of common traditions in the Bible. Further, many Christians find even that omission difficult so they employ a euphemism, "In your name we pray." Why one would pray to God in God's name is not made clear. Of course "your name" is intended to refer to Jesus.[32]

In point of fact, a truly nonsectarian prayer is an impossibility in a pluralistic democracy. Since the atheist has no target for prayer, prayer is simply not possible. For her or him "nonsectarian" prayer is "no" prayer.

But let us examine a specific example of a public prayer. Following are some excerpts from *Prayers Offered by the Chaplain*,[33] a volume of prayers delivered at the opening of Senate sessions from 1961 to 1964. Frederick Brown Harris was the resident chaplain for the Senate during that period. He was a Protestant and presumably felt that his prayers touched a chord with the majority. He clearly had no concern about what his prayers might say to Sens. Jacob Javits and Abraham Ribicoff. On Wednesday, June 20, 1962, within a week of the *Engel* decision, Harris prayed, "So that the gates of this realm of wonder, closed to the merely clever and conceited, may be opened unto us as we turn to Thee, our God, in the simplicity as it is in Christ, our Lord. In His spirit and in His passion for others, strengthen us to dedicate all we have and are to help heal the open sores of the stricken earth. In His name we ask it. Amen." Or again, on June 23 Harris closed with, "In the name of the risen Redeemer, who declares, 'Because I live, ye, too, shall live.' Amen." Finally, the day after *Engel* Harris blithely prayed, "We ask it in the name of Him who is the way, the truth, and the life."

To be sure there were only two Jews in the Senate, so why

should the ninety and eight not pray their druthers? While they were at it, why not engage in regular sexist banter since there was only one female in the chamber?

The Final Week of Hearings, 1964

On May 27 Professor Philip Kurland of the University of Chicago Law School testified quite effectively against the Becker amendment. But the highlight of his appearance was the little-known quote from a speech in 1924 by President Coolidge: "Some people do not seem to understand fully the purpose of our constitutional restraints. They are not for protecting the majority, either in or out of Congress. They can protect themselves with their votes. We have adopted a written Constitution in order that the minority even down to the most insignificant individual, might have their rights protected."[34]

Just prior to the final session of the committee William Randolph Hearst weighed in with a long editorial in which he suggested, "Let those who don't want God in their lives try to evade Him. Clarifying the legality of voluntary and nonsectarian public prayer merely restores the rights of the rest of us—who do want God in our lives."[35] But the tide had turned. The concerted effort of the mainstream churches and the failure of persons like Graham and Peale to claim the stage on behalf of amendments combined to sink Becker's hopes. It is also reasonable to assume that the scores of separate amendments offered by more than 150 representatives tended to dissipate the strength Becker had mustered. Those same persons who signed the discharge petition often wasted important committee time discussing the merits of alternative language. Beyond this was the fact that President Kennedy strongly endorsed the Court action, as did the United

States solicitor general in the summer of 1963. President Johnson did nothing to alter the administration's public posture in 1964. And, finally, there was the master stroke of 223 constitutional law professors filing a statement opposing the Becker amendment five days after the last hearings were held. The statement was entitled, "Our Most Precious Heritage."[36]

It was obvious that Celler had no intention of letting the Becker amendment reach the floor. In April Becker had the upper hand by a few votes, according to the count of Dean Kelley. By the time the hearings ended the count was reversed. Becker's last hope, the discharge petition, remained some fifty votes short of the number required. Writing about the events in 1969 in his book *School Prayer*, John Laubach penned this obituary for the 1964 prayer amendment efforts.

> Congressman Becker introduced his last lament into the *Congressional Record* as the 1964 session came to an end. Recognizing the support he had received from four of five American Cardinals, and of thirty-six of fifty-five Bishops who had replied to his inquiries, he remarked, "However, this session comes to an end without the Congress taking any action on my constitutional amendment . . . I regret this more than I can put in words, and while I will not return to Congress next year, I shall not cease in my efforts to restore a 173-year right to the American people."[37]

Notes

1. Religious News Service, April 18, 1964, dateline Atlanta.

2. As I have examined in detail the three volumes of testimony garnered by the committee the analysis of that material by John Herbert

Laubach has been most helpful. In his book *School Prayer: Congress, the Courts, and the Public* (Public Affairs Press, 1969), he offered a thorough analysis of the two most prominent constitutional amendments proposed in the 1960s—the Becker and the Dirksen efforts.

3. U.S. Congress, House, Hearings Before the Committee on the Judiciary, *School Prayers* (Washington, D.C.: U.S. Government Printing Office, 1964), vol. 1, p. 213. This three-volume record contains all testimony, letters, and research material related to the subject under consideration. There were eighteen days of hearings stretching from April 22 to June 3.

4. Ibid., p. 220.

5. Ibid., p. 229. It is interesting that Graham would list all the ills he saw in society as somehow resulting from two Supreme Court decisions within the last two years.

6. U.S. Congress, House Hearings, *School Prayers*, p. 239.

7. Rev. Bernard Braskamp, D.D., *Prayers Offered by the Chaplain* (Washington, D.C.: U.S. Government Printing Office, 1965), p. 196. Rev. Frederick Brown Harris, D.D., LL.D., LITT.D., *Prayers Offered by the Chaplain* (Washington, D.C.: U.S. Government Printing Office, 1964), pp. 265, 191. The first volume was printed by order of the House at government expense, the second by order of the Senate at government expense. As a result of a suit filed in the 1980s by Professor Paul Kurtz of the State University of New York at Buffalo, printing of the prayers at government expense has, we understand, ceased.

8. U.S. Congress, House Hearings, *School Prayers*, vol. 1, p. 257.

9. Ibid., p. 273.

10. Ibid., p. 282.

11. Ibid., p. 313.

12. Ibid., pp. 283–84.

13. Ibid., p. 344.

14. Ibid., p. 352.

15. Ibid., p. 421.

16. Ibid., p. 506.

17. Ibid., pp. 536–37

18. Ibid., p. 656.

19. Ibid., p. 676.

20. Ibid., pp. 656-57. In an extended commentary Tuller offered this particularly cogent argument.

I fear state religion. My heritage is definitely rooted in this particular background. I feel that if the people of the United States wish to undergird their personal lives and their social life by the power of prayer and Bible reading they have through the free exercise clause not only the right but the responsibility so to do.

The place for this, sir, in my opinion, is in the homes of our country and in the churches and religious institutions. It is not in the public schools. This is the contention that I am placing strongly before you. If the public schools are to be used as an agency for evangelism or religious education, sir, I think they would tend to weaken rather than strengthen the strong religious witness we have in these United States.

I believe strongly that the strength of our religious heritage among the common people of the United States is posited upon the voluntary nature of such religious conviction; that it would be seriously damaged through any effort of the State to bolster, or strengthen it through these procedures. (p. 665)

21. Ibid., p. 667.

22. Ibid., p. 711.

23. Ibid., p. 841.

24. Ibid., pp. 923-24.

25. Robert S. Alley, "The Television Church," in *TV Genres,* ed. Brian Rose (Westport, Conn.: Greenwood Press), p. 399.

26. U.S. Congress, House Hearings, *School Prayers,* vol. 2, p. 1367.

27. Ibid., p. 1584.

28. Ibid., p. 1752.

29. The committee took the better part of a week off after the hearings on May 21. During that time all the various Baptist conventions in the United States gathered in Atlantic City for a 150th year celebration of the organization of Baptists in the United States. Each of the

conventions represented held separate business sessions prior to joint celebration on the weekend. Southern Baptists, by far the largest group, routinely addressed a report of its resolutions committee on Friday morning. Its report would have maintained opposition to prayer amendments. However, a Richmond minister, J. Levering Evans, moved to amend the religious liberty resolution so as to endorse school prayer. Apparently stunned, committee members made no response and "without giving the opposition a chance to speak, the convention president at the demand of 'question' put the matter to a vote" (*Washington Post,* May 23, 1964). The motion carried by a narrow margin. "Thereupon, Reuben E. Alley, editor of the *Religious Herald* of Richmond, moved reconsideration. His paper, along with other Southern Baptist papers, had been outspoken against the Becker amendment as a threat to religious liberty. Since he had voted for the Evans motion, he was eligible to ask reconsideration. [Alley had cast his vote with the majority for that very purpose, since he saw it as the only parliamentary action available to him if he desired to be heard on the matter.] 'It's my opinion,' he declared, 'that nothing has come before this convention, or will come before it in the foreseeable future, that's so important as this. By passing this, you would authorize paid agents of your State to come into your public schools and conduct worship' " (*Washington Post,* May 23, 1964). Faced with a sobered convention Evans asked to amend his own motion so as to oppose "any further amendment to the Constitution respecting establishment of religion or free exercise thereof." It was passed nearly unanimously.

The convention was bookended by Rep. Eugene Siler, who spoke to the convention on Wednesday afternoon, and Billy Graham, who closed the Friday morning session with a sermon advising the country to "jump into the Vietnam conflict with both feet—or pull our entirely." Both men were strong advocates of the Becker amendment. That was the dilemma for the leaders who wished to hold the traditional support for strict separation of church and state. But the wave of fundamentalism that has now engulfed the convention was still of relatively small influence in policy. The convention was usually regaled with blood and thunder sermons, in between which the moderates directed daily activity and charted a course of commitment to religious freedom. By 1982 the situation was reversed and Vice President Bush, an Episcopalian with no reason to insert his advice, spoke to the convention in session in New Orleans urging Southern Baptists to help pass the prayer amendment. In that year the convention departed from its opposition to such amendments and roundly endorsed the Republican-led effort to "put God back in the schools."

It is difficult to assess the importance of the 1964 Atlantic City meeting. No one can be certain what effect an endorsement of the Becker amendment by the largest Protestant denomination in the country might have had on the House committee when it reconvened on May 27. The record shows intense questioning of C. Emanuel Carlson, director of the Baptist Joint Committee on Public Affairs, about the incident. Rep. Richard Poff of Virginia pointedly asked, "I believe the Southern Baptists Convention considered an amendment to that resolution offered by a delegate from Richmond, did it not? . . . They adopted that amendment, did they not?" Carlson's response was bumbling, a result of poor preparation. Chairman Celler informed the committee that a *Washington Post* account of the events in Atlantic City was in the record (p. 2109). That led Poff to press further. After an exchange of misinformation the matter was dropped. Had there been a clearcut endorsement of Becker by the Southern Baptist Convention the discussion would likely have taken a different turn. But that is speculative.

30. *The Religious Herald.*

31. See the 1992 *Weisman* case discussed in chapter 11.

32. A remarkably well-argued statement on this subject was made by Rabbi Seymour Siegel of the Jewish Theological Seminary of America. He testified at the 1982 Senate hearings convened to examine S.J. Res. 199, President Reagan's prayer amendment. Rabbi Siegel favored S.J. Res. 199. He was asked by Sen. Jeremiah Denton of Alabama whether a prayer approved by the Alabama governor for possible use in the public schools was offensive. It closed, "in the name of our Lord. Amen." The rabbi replied, "This is even an example of a watering down which

is not even a watering down, because the last phrase, 'in the name of our Lord,' or 'the Lord,' could be—in fact, I think is—not offensive, but objectionable to Jews, because it is obviously an echo of the proper Christian formula which Christians should use, as I think Jesus instructed Christians to pray in his name. Even though it doesn't mention the name of Jesus, it does imply that, or at least have the echo of the traditional Christian formula, because otherwise, if you are praying, you are obviously praying in the name of God" (Senate Hearings 1982, p. 125).

33. Rev., Frederick Brown Harris, *Prayers Offered by the Chaplain.*

34. U.S. Congress, House Hearings, *School Prayers*, vol. 3, p. 2153.

35. Ibid., p. 2394.

36. Ibid., pp. 2483–87.

37. John Herbert Laubach, *School Prayer* (Washington, D.C.: Public Affairs Press, 1969).

9

Senate Hearings, 1966

In January 1966 Sen. Everett Dirksen of Illinois, speaking to a journalism fraternity, Sigma Delta Chi, asserted, "I'm not going to let nine men say to 190 million people, including children, when and where they can utter prayers." He continued, "The high and august Court put thumbs down on prayer." In response, the *Washington Post* observed, "The high and august Court did no such thing, . . . It protected the freedom of 190 million people, including children, to pray exactly when and how they pleased . . . by asserting that no governmental authority may prescribe a prayer or other form of worship in any public school."

It was the opening salvo of efforts by Dirksen to accomplish what the House had failed to effect in 1964. On March 22 he introduced his constitutional amendment saying that it was something "sooner or later, Congress must come to grips with." It is "quite clear," and "simple," Dirksen told the Senate. "Shall the people be afforded an opportunity to act on language which will clarify this vexing problem before it is carried to ridiculous extremes by other suits which may be filed?"

In May Rep. William Cramer of Florida proposed a constitutional amendment that would "prevent any interpretation of the Constitution that might prohibit the federal or state governments from referring to or relying upon God in conducting the business of government." Cramer's language resulted from work with an ad hoc committee created by fifty members of the House "who are particularly interested in the problem." The Floridian stated that his amendment "calls for a redeclaration by all Americans that we are, always have been, and will continue to be, a nation under God." The House failed to act on this proposed legislation.

On August 1, 1966, Sen. Birch Bayh of Indiana convened his Senate subcommittee on constitutional amendments to begin six days of hearings on Dirksen's Senate Joint Resolution 148. The resolution read as follows:

Section 1. Nothing contained in this Constitution shall prohibit the authority administering any school, educational institution or other public building supported in whole or in part through the expenditure of public funds from providing for or permitting the voluntary participation by students or others in prayer. Nothing contained in this article shall authorize any such authority to prescribe the form or content of any prayer.

Bayh's subcommittee of the Senate Committee on the Judiciary had six Democratic members and three Republican. Only three of the nine legislators attended any sessions. Bayh was present for all six days. Sen. Joseph Tydings of Maryland and Sen. Roman Hruska of Nebraska each attended three days. This lack of involvement by committee members in the face of the signatures of forty-eight senators sponsoring the Dirksen amendment may suggest that everyone knew the futility of the exercise. The number of votes required, sixty-seven, just did not appear to be there.

Even so, Bayh moved valiantly on. His committee heard twenty-two statements in opposition to the amendment and seventeen in favor. Many of the same persons who had testified at the House hearings in 1964 reappeared for this second inquiry. Dirksen spoke first.

As I went through that [Testimony before the House in 1964] it occurred to me that somehow we had had every sophisticated argument except an argument from the common man of this country, who was defined as one who works and prays and pays his bills and goes to church, rears a family in decency as law-abiding children. Strange, in all this, we have not heard from any of those, and we are beginning to hear from him by the millions, and he is going to have his say.[1]

Dirksen engaged Father Robert Drinan, Dean of Boston College Law School, in a brief exchange. Toward the end of his testimony Drinan commented, "Children do not get together and pray voluntarily. If they do that, it is arranged or provided for by a church, some religious organization, or by the school. I think that the proposal . . . omitting 'provided for' would be even more meaningless and needless than the present article."[2] Drinan was making the point that the amendment without those two words suggests that school systems "are now forbidding voluntary participation by students in prayer, and I think that that is an illusion."

From that time until the end of the hearings the committee was engaged largely in a protracted exploration of the meaning of "voluntary." The most prolonged exchange (eighty pages of testimony) took place on the first afternoon, with the appearance of Bertram Daiker, attorney for the school board in the *Engel*

case, and Edward Bazarian, attorney for plaintiffs in *Stein* v.
Oshinsky.[3]

In the discussion with Daiker the question arose as to which
school official would prescribe the content of a prayer under
the Dirksen amendment. The answer was that none could. At
that point Bayh quoted from a recent *Washington Post* article,
"Dirksen Sees PTA's Directing Schools Voluntary Prayer." The
Post reported that Dirksen "pictured the PTAs yesterday as the
authority directing children's prayer if his proposed 'voluntary
prayer' amendment to the constitution is adopted."[4] Daiker then
argued that the PTA was not an authority so it could prescribe
a prayer.

The whole problem at that point was the clear fact that if
prayer was to be organized then someone or some group must
decide its content. The ruse that the PTA could perform this
function because it was not an official state organization begs
the question of how the authorized prayer becomes a part of
the classroom agenda. There was no escape that ultimately the
teacher had to make decisions about events in the classroom.
Would she or he be free to reject a PTA authorized prayer? If
not, would not her acceptance of it make him or her the authorizing
agent? It is fair to say there was no meeting of the minds on
this conflict.

As the committee turned to Bazarian attention remained upon
the question of definition of "voluntary." Bazarian asserted that,
"It would be the function of the school board to set up a procedural
technique whereby the voluntary prayer program could be
accomplished procedurally."[5]

Well, of course the very word "procedural" raises serious
doubt about the meaning of "voluntary." It was clear that proponents of the Dirksen amendment saw "voluntary" as meaning the ability to absent oneself from the procedures. This comes

out in Bazarian's suggestion that, "The school board might well say that the first ten minutes of each day can be devoted to religious exercises." That itself is a prescription by the board forbidden by the Dirksen amendment. And the opportunity to absent oneself from prayer is not an opportunity voluntarily accepted. It is a choice forced upon the dissenter, who must then volunteer within the parameters of school board policy.

C. Emanuel Carlson, representing Baptists, offered a helpful definition when he observed:

> Voluntary, if it is to be significant then, must have the personal element. It is the person who has the freedom of exercise, not the authority, and to talk about voluntary prayer under the operations of a school authority is, I think, an oxymoron. . . . It is internally contradictory to have an authority arranging for voluntarism. The no restraint or free exercise concept of the First Amendment simply stops government here.[6]

Leo Pfeffer put it bluntly two days later. "It is not permissible for the school teacher even acting individually but acting by virtue of, under color of, law, . . . to say 'Children, we will now pray.' The teacher can say that only because she is the voice of the State."[7]

Clyde Taylor, general director of the National Association of Evangelicals, speaking for the Dirksen amendment, understood this quite clearly. He said, "I think there is no doubt about it that the school superintendent would have to be involved, because a school is a section of ordered society. It has rules and regulations. It has a curriculum, and they just couldn't insert prayer or Bible reading wherever, as we sometimes say in religious circles, the spirit moves them. There has to be some order here."[8]

As the end of the fifth day approached it was left to Robert

Bennett, minister of a Baptist Church in Washington, to enunciate what lay behind the beliefs of almost all those who, like him, wanted the Dirksen amendment. He said quite honestly, "These young people need to know the Creator of the universe. If you can help them in this, it is your responsibility to the citizens you represent to do so."[9] Behind all the argument lay a fundamental and clear division between those who envisioned the United States as a Christian nation with a mission from God and those who saw the nation as a secular state with religion outside its purview. And that is why advocates prescribing "voluntary prayer" find a moment of silence self-defeating. Speaking on the final afternoon for the American Legion, Daniel O'Connor made this clear. "Senator, the period of silence would be the direct victory of those who fought against the school prayer, because they do not want the name of Almighty God orally mentioned in public prayer."[10] Another O'Connor, Justice Sandra Day, gave the appropriate constitutional response to the American Legion representative in her concurring opinion in *Wallace v. Jaffree* (1985).[11]

A Personal Experience—August 8, 1966

On Monday afternoon, August 8, my wife Norma and I entered the Senate Office Building and went to the hearing room where the subcommittee on constitutional amendments was holding hearings on the Dirksen Amendment concerning school prayer. As we entered representatives from the American Legion were making an impassioned plea for the Dirksen plan. Cameras rolled and reporters recorded the dialogue with Sen. Bayh. As soon as the Legion concluded the cameras and newspeople departed, as did most of the audience. A skeleton staff and Bayh remained.

The hour was late but the chairman was gracious. He had invited me to testify and he offered me the time to do so.

The room was like a tomb. I recalled my last visit to that building, more than ten years before, when Sen. Joseph McCarthy was baiting the army. I spent an entire day observing, along with an overflowing crowd, the drama that was to be McCarthy's downfall. As I responded to Bayh's questions I was mindful that much of the McCarthy spirit was fueling this newest attack upon minority rights in the name of patriotism. My formal remarks of that afternoon were based upon the same Madisonian principles set forth in the introduction to this book, but coming as they did in the heat of the conflict, the words have a certain sixties ring. Since I was privileged to have the "last word" in public testimony before the hearings concluded, I have taken the author's option to reproduce those remarks in appendix B.

Senator Bayh seemed rather relaxed as the three of us walked out of the hearing room at the close of the session. He assured me that he was thoroughly committed to the defeat of the Dirksen amendment,[12] but he feared that in an election year it was going to be difficult to convince colleagues to "vote against God." So, he said, I should not be surprised if he sponsored a Senate resolution favoring voluntary prayer. He went on to explain that through such an action he would hope to give at least a few senators an alternative pro-God vote, thus eroding the clearly existing Dirksen majority. Since the amendment required two-thirds of the senators to vote in the affirmative, Bayh was reasonably sure his tactics would assure denial of the sixty-seven votes needed for passage.

The *Congressional Record* offers a detailed description of Bayh's strategy. Dirksen sensed he was going to lose in both the subcommittee and the full committee, so he threatened to force his amendment to the Senate floor after Labor Day by asking to substitute his proposal for a resolution endorsing UNICEF. In response the Bayh committee reported the Dirksen amendment to the Judiciary Committee without recommendation. Due in part to the absence of three Dirksen supporters, the full committee did not report the amendment to the full Senate.

With no report from the Judiciary Committee, on September 19 the Senate agreed to take up the Dirksen Amendment in place of the UNICEF resolution. It was at that point that Senator Bayh introduced a sense-of-the-Senate resolution endorsing voluntary prayer.

Whereas the Supreme Court of the United States has decided that it is a violation of the constitutional prohibition against the establishment of religion for a state authority to prescribe and require religious practices in public schools; and

Whereas these decisions have been widely misrepresented, misinterpreted and misunderstood; and

Whereas the Supreme Court decisions did not involve or prohibit voluntary prayer or silent meditation in our public schools, or spontaneous prayer in our public schools during time of tragedy; or public school programs commemorating religious events of traditional and historical significance; or the offering of prayer in various public ceremonies involving adults; or references to God on our coins or in our historical documents and patriotic songs; and Whereas the Supreme Court decisions acknowledged that we are a religious people whose institutions presuppose a Supreme Being: Now, therefore, be it

Resolved by the Senate and House of Representatives of the United States of America in Congress assembled, That it is the sense of the Congress that nothing in the Constitution or the Supreme Court decisions relating to religious practices in our public schools prohibits local school official from permitting individual students to engage in silent, voluntary prayer or meditation; and

Be it further resolved, That the President of the United States is requested and authorized to issue annually a proclamation designating the week during which Thanksgiving Day is observed as National Prayer and Meditation Week, inviting the Governors and mayors of State and local governments of the United States to issue similar proclamations, and urging all Americans, both adults and children, to express, during this period, their thanks for the numerous blessings which have been granted to all the people of the United States.[13]

Opponents of the Bayh alternative quickly identified its danger to their cause. Sen. Hruska chided Bayh. "It means nothing. It will give a good many Senators a chance to vote for God, for country, and for home, so that they can return to their respective States and say, 'Yes, I favored the sense-of-Congress resolution. Therefore, I am on the side of prayer and belief in God, and that this is a religious Nation,' and so on. That it will do. But it certainly does not mean a thing legally; nor will it have any binding effect on anyone."[14]

Of course Hruska was correct and Bayh knew it. In response he stated, "I feel the proposal would have a wholesome result as far as clarifying and stilling some of the confusion and controversy which have risen. It is to this goal that we have been directing support for a sense-of-Congress resolution, not a desire for anyone to be able to say he is in favor of motherhood and God, although that might be the inference taken with respect to it."

In the typical atmosphere of senatorial courtesy, Sen. Hruska responded, "Before we go further, let the senator from Indiana be dispossessed of the thought that the senator from Nebraska charged the senator from Indiana with proposing the sense-of-

Congress resolution with that motive."[15]

The debate on the floor, the opposition led by Senators Bayh and Sam Ervin, lasted for three days and resulted in a vote of forty-nine votes for the Dirksen amendment, thirty-seven against. Had all fourteen nonvoting senators voted with Dirksen it would not have helped. The opposition required only thirty-four nays.

The breakdown of the votes tells an interesting story. Thirty-three senators voted "yea" on the Bayh resolution. Three others senators who were absent were paired with other colleagues and would have voted "yea." The maximum number for Bayh would appear to have been thirty-six. Of those that voted for Bayh twenty-eight voted against Dirksen. Turning to that amendment, thirty-seven Senators voted "nay," and one other would have voted in the negative. Of those senators who voted "nay" nine opposed the Bayh substitute. On the other hand there were five senators who voted for Bayh and then for Dirksen. There is little purpose in speculating about those twenty-eight senators who first endorsed Bayh and then helped defeat Dirksen. If twenty of them, absent the Bayh choice, had switched to support of the Dirksen Amendment, it would have prevailed. But none, of course, would likely have admitted taking the option Hruska identified in his remarks.

As Bayh talked quietly about his plans on that August afternoon I was reminded of a similar strategy used by James Madison in his effort to defeat the General Assessment Bill in the Virginia legislature in 1784. As the reader will recall, Madison was faced with two bills offensive to him, assessment and Episcopal establishment.[16] He admitted to his father parrying the assessment bill for the moment by voting for establishment.[17]

Notes

1. U.S. Congress, Senate Hearings before the Subcommittee on Constitutional Amendments, *School Prayers* (Washington, D.C.: U.S. Government Printing Office, 1966), p. 13.

2. Ibid., p. 22.

3. In that case the circuit court examined the fact that the principal of the school, Oshinsky, had ruled there would be no prayer in the school. In its decision the court found that it is the responsibility of the school authorities to determine the curriculum, not the parents. The long discussion between Bazarian and Bayh stuck on that point. Bazarian insisted that "the state in the preferment of those, in banning prayer, preferred those who did not believe over those who do. Bayh and Sen. Tydings asserted the chief issue was who was going to determine the curriculum, the school board or the parents. The parents contended that the refusal of the school authorities to facilitate the prayers was a denial of free exercise.

4. U.S. Congress, Senate Hearings, *School Prayers*, p. 81.

5. Ibid., p. 204.

6. Ibid., p. 248.

7. Ibid., p. 352.

8. Ibid., p. 437.

9. Ibid., p. 483.

10. Ibid., p. 547.

11. See *Wallace* v. *Jaffree*, concurring opinion by Justice O'Connor. "The Court does not hold that the Establishment Clause is so hostile to religion that it precludes the States from affording schoolchildren an opportunity for voluntary prayer. To the contrary, the moment of silence statutes of many States should satisfy the Establishment Clause standard we have here applied. The Court holds only that Alabama has intentionally crossed the line between creating a quiet moment during which those so inclined may pray, and affirmatively endorsing the particular religious practice of prayer."

12. Later commentary on the events tended to link Bayh with

Dirksen because few observers took the time to examine the evidence.

13. *Congressional Record*, Senate, 87th Congress, 2nd Session, September 20, 1966, p. 23161.

14. Ibid., p. 23158.

15. Ibid., p. 23159.

16. See above, p. 27.

17. "Letter from James Madison, Jr., to James Madison, Sr., January 6, 1785," in *The Papers of James Madison,* ed. Robert Rutland and William M. E. Rachal, vol. 8 (Chicago: University of Chicago Press, 1973).

10

House Debate, 1971

The House in Session

Throughout the months of 1971 pressure mounted in the House of Representatives for yet another try at an amendment to the Bill of Rights. The chair of the House Judiciary Committee consistently refused to hold further hearings on the matter, pointing to the exhaustive eighteen days of testimony in 1964. Finally, on November 8, 1971, the requisite number of representatives had signed on to a discharge petition and Rep. Chalmers Wylie of Ohio called up a motion to discharge the further consideration of House Joint Resolution 191 by the Committee on the Judiciary. Wylie went into the ensuing debate with a majority of the House supporting his constitutional amendment.

Section 1. Nothing contained in this Constitution shall abridge the right of persons lawfully assembled, in any public building which is supported in whole or in part through the expenditure of public funds, to participate in nondenominational prayer.

The House session for Monday, November 8, 1971, was opened by the chaplain, the Rev. Edward Latch, with a quote from the book of Luke in the New Testament: "Lord teach us to pray, and he said unto them, When you pray, say, Our Father." Not too subtly, Latch then intoned, "With the coming of another week, our Father, we pause at the altar of prayer, founded by our fathers, that we may be strengthened with might by Thy spirit to face the tasks of these hours with faith and hope and love." Latch knew a denominational prayer when he wrote one. It is interesting that he attributed to the Founders the establishment of an altar of prayer, considering that the Constitutional Convention refused to hire a chaplain to open each day with prayer even as its members were writing the Constitution.

Wylie began the debate by urging immediate consideration and passage. Rep. Celler opposed the discharge, reminding the House that in 1964 the hearings had dealt with thirty-five different forms of the current resolution. It failed then and it was, he noted, impossible now to write such a bill on the floor, bypassing committee procedures. After a few more minutes the discharge was voted upon and passed 242 to 157 with 32 not voting. Having been brought to the floor, passage of the prayer amendment would require 288 votes, or, put otherwise, it would take 144 votes in the negative to defeat. Managers of the amendment knew they lacked the votes and indeed when, at the end of the debate, the roll call was held only 240 voted for the Wylie resolution.

The debate was spirited and of a different tone than that witnessed in the sixties. Primarily this was the result of admission by proponents that they needed to trim the original purpose of overturning *Engel* by merely affirming the individual's right to pray in a public building. Apart from the fact that no such restriction existed, it was a recognition that the more aggressive approach of Dirksen and Becker would not work. Rep.

Montgomery of Mississippi made this clear early in the debate. "What the American people are interested in is that the Supreme Court has restricted prayer in public schools and they do not like it one bit. If the people want voluntary prayer in the public schools and we represent the people, then I think we should approve this resolution."

This was a deft switching of grounds. On its face, nothing in the resolution overturned the Supreme Court restrictions. It merely affirmed that which had never been denied. The congressman went on to the political realities acknowledged by Sen. Bayh in 1966. "Let us lay our cards on the table. A vote for the proposed constitutional amendment is going to be a lot easier to explain back home than a vote against it. I know that if I vote against the resolution today, my opponent next year will make me do a lot of explaining."[1]

Early on the word "nondenominational" came under fire as possibly prohibiting denominational prayer in public buildings. Of course this critic had caught the heart of the matter. Whatever the resolution stated on its face, it was designed to establish identifiable, programmed, audible prayers. The term was a revised version of Billy Graham's nonsectarian prayer of 1966.

Rep. McCulloch of Ohio made this point when he reminded his colleagues, "Since force of law is totally unnecessary to cause voluntary prayer to be said, the resolution must be intended to cause some people to pray who really do not want to pray."[2]

Celler came directly to the point in his opening remarks, noting, "It is impossible to devise a meaningful prayer which would be nondenominational or nonsectarian so that it would not invade some basic tenet of religious practice." Quoting from the *Catholic Times*, Celler affirmed, "The bill in question has remained in committee because no one could resolve the question, 'What does a non-denominational prayer look like?' The answer is, of course, no one knows, because it is impossible to compose a prayer that is not denominational."[3]

From the beginning the debate was confused because there lay in the wings an amendment by John Buchanan of Alabama that would replace "nondenominational" with the words "participate in voluntary prayer and meditation." Under the rules Rep. Wylie had control over what amendments would be allowed and he accepted only the Buchanan alternative. It was clear that prayer proponents were playing word games in order to accomplish their objective. Since 1962 they had gone fom supporting prescribed prayer in public schools, to prayer, to nonsectarian prayer, to nondenominational prayer, to voluntary prayer, to a voluntary moment of silence.[4]

That explains why Rep. Reid of New York asked the key question about the definition of "voluntary" when he inquired, "Would not even voluntary prayer involve the state in the sponsoring of a religious exercise by its providing classroom space and designating a period during official school hours for prayer?"[5]

In spite of the Buchanan amendment the first hours of debate that morning were focused on the original language, including "nondenominational."[6] Rep. Wylie, the sponsor of the discharge petition, responded to certain inquiries from Rep. Sam Gibbons about nondenominational prayer. Gibbons asked, "Who is to determine what is a nondenominational prayer?" Wylie replied, "The local school authorities would determine this, subject to judicial review, which should be exercised in the event those authorities clearly abuse their discretion."[7]

Wylie's reply to Gibbons's third question reveals exactly what he meant by "voluntary." Question: "Who in the school will give the prayer?" Answer: "The person giving the prayer should be a volunteer from among the faculty, administration or student body of the school. Clearly, no person could be compelled to give the prayer or otherwise participate."

Gibbons asked, "Does your amendment envision that a school board should prescribe a certain prayer of their choosing as being the nondenominational prayer for their school system?" Wylie responded, "Not necessarily. It could be composed by a student. It could be the prayer from the *Engel* case, which the Supreme Court said was nondenominational, or it could be the prayer of the Senate or House Chaplain. A local school board would have the power to say that prayer is not nondenominational, I would think." One wonders whether the prayer of the House chaplain, given three days after the *Engel* decision, would qualify:

> Thou who wert the God of the Founding Fathers and all their succeeding generations, may we never become careless of the legacy of faith and the inheritance of inspiration which they have bequeathed to us.
>
> We earnestly beseech Thee that in these times of consternation and confusion we may have such a clear and commanding vision of their longings and labor, their prayers and petitions to make this a God-fearing nation, that we shall follow and obey that vision with all the passion and perseverance of our minds and hearts.
>
> Grant that, inspired by our deepest instincts and noblest impulses, we may be brave and courageous in rejecting the creed of a godless adversary and zealously reaffirm our faith in the spiritual values of prayer which are equal to all the dark and dismal moods which are hovering over the souls of many in our day.
>
> Hear us in the name of the Prince of Peace. Amen.[8]

As the debate continued Rep. Robert Drinan of Massachusetts had this to say about the label "nondenominational."

There is no satisfactory definition of the term "nondenomina-tional." Even if, furthermore, the particular term "nondenom-inational" is omitted from the proposed amendment to the Bill of Rights any prayer sought to be justified under the First Amendment of the Constitution must in the nature of things be nonsectarian or "subdenominational" or "sub-Christian." The very concept of prayer seems inevitably to include a theistic element. It is precisely because of this element that any prayer must be deemed to reflect the theology of a particular group and is consequently denominational or sectarian.[9]

Drinan continued with this characterization of the proposed amendment:

Today's amendment seeks to create an ersatz religion. Today's proposal in short suggests that the Government in the person of the teacher, the school board or the courts move in upon our public schools by certifying or approving that a particular prayer is indeed "nondenominational." . . . The Wylie amend-ment states that the public schools, while outlawing all real religious exercises now engaged in by Americans, must invent, import, and establish some novel religious exercise not taken from any one individual denomination but gathered from all religions into a composite prayer unacceptable to the members of all denominations but acceptable to the Government which has sanctioned the practice.

The opponents of the amendment, under the leadership of Reps. Cellar and Corman, concluded their remarks and the focus turned to Wylie. His first speaker, Rep. Waggonner of Louisiana, suggested that freedom of religion had been "trampled on by the Supreme Court." For his part, "The greatest freedom we enjoy and which has to be protected at all costs is that freedom which was paid for on Calvary's Cross. I believe that the cause of the living God is best served by passing this proposed amendment." Then, apparently speaking for the leadership, he noted that the word "nondenominational" was to be removed and replaced by Buchanan's language.

Rep. Hunt of New Jersey was concerned that a spiritual heritage must be imparted to the nation's children. He viewed the Court's actions as devaluing religious values and enhancing "temporal values devoid of any spiritual consistency."[10] Waggonner was satisfied that the juvenile delinquency rampant in the nation could be, to some degree, abated by school prayer. Rep. Carter of Kentucky spoke to the term "nondenominational," insisting that the Lord's Prayer was such a prayer. The full force of the delinquency argument was advanced by Rep. Thompson of Georgia. "If we look back on the moral attitude of the students before the Supreme Court decision, which had the effect of outlawing prayer, and compare it with the attitude as it exists today, we can only conclude that with the Court-ordered removal of the student's right to pray to God in school that drugs, crime, and filthy books have all increased on the school campuses. In short, the moral fiber of our school students has been eroded. We need to put God back into the lives of students and this amendment will help to do that."[11]

After further extended debate Rep. Jacobs offered the following amendment, "strike 'participate in nondenominational prayer' and insert 'observe a moment of silence, each in his own way.'"[12] It is interesting to speculate how one observes a moment of silence in his own way. In any event, the motion was out of order.

Most of Wylie's supporters made a great deal out of numerous polls that indicated overwhelming public support for his amendment. "This amendment has recently been subject to a great deal of criticism from national religious leaders, among others. However, several polls have shown that the rank and file members of these religious groups strongly support the prayer amendment and oppose the views expressed for their organization."[13] There is ample evidence to support this contention, but the results are clouded by the public misperceptions about what the Court had actually done and what was permitted in the schools.

Rep. Don Edwards of California introduced a series of observations by Professor Charles Black of the Yale Law School.[14] The argument advanced by the legal scholar went to the heart of the matter at the time and should be required reading for those who continue, under other, more innocuous language, to perpetuate the same arguments for prayer.

As the debate progressed an interesting fact emerged for public assessment. Rep. Vanik, an opponent of the amendment, complained that the leadership had allowed only amendments to the original that were agreeable to Wylie to be introduced.

> Under the procedure, the author of the amendment has the sole and exclusive power to permit an amendment to his proposal. It was a master stroke that prevented moderates from altering the amendment until it was acceptable to them, possibly retaining the hard core support of those committed to the original. The House leadership gave no opportunity to tinker with the resolution until it could garner the two-thirds vote required. It was assumed that its sponsor would not suggest "gutting" amendments.

Indeed, as noted above, Wylie accepted only one "perfecting" amendment. The House knew about it but it had not yet been presented by Rep. John Buchanan of Alabama.

The debate then turned to that change even before it was

offered. Rep. Gray noted the existence of the House chaplain and asked, "Would we be opposed to allowing schoolchildren to have this same love and respect for their Maker as adults? This is particularly true since the so-called nondenominational prayer has been stricken by an amendment changing the word to 'voluntary' from 'nondenominational.' "[15] Gray also read a letter from Billy Graham stating:

> I do not believe the Constitutional Amendment jeopardizes the historical separation of church and state as some have alleged. Our greatest danger lies in the direction that secularism and atheism may become the unofficial religion of America. I see no danger in the Amendment. If I were a Congressman I would vote for it. I believe that the overwhelming majority of the American people want prayer in the schools.

One member reminded the Congress, "The first colonists who settled on these shores did so in flight from oppressive established religions in the old world."[16] The facts tell another story. Virginia was the first settlement and established in that colony the same "oppressive" regime that existed in England. Similarly, almost all of the colonies of the seventeenth century established some form of Christianity.

Rep. Don Clausen noted that he would have had to oppose the amendment until the change by Buchanan was approved. Several other congressmen agreed, noting that the term "nondenominational sanctions nonreligious prayer in schools." The substance of the arguments made by the many representatives who agreed to support the amendment boiled down to, "While I opposed the original form of the 'nondenominational' resolution, I support the 'voluntary prayer and meditation' resolution as amended."[17]

Finally Buchanan introduced his change, substitution of the word "voluntary." As the debate progressed it was clear that a number of members were much more at ease with the new language. Rep. White of Texas noted, "I think it is imperative to change the word 'nondenominational' to 'voluntary' because it is difficult if not impossible to define nondenominational."[18]

The opposition quickly rallied to respond to Buchanan. Rep. Mikva of Illinois offered these thoughts: "But is it voluntary when you talk about the child who must be in school because of compulsory attendance law and must stand there in silent prayer or not praying as he or she wishes?"[19] Mikva then noted that if it's not nondenominational then it must be denominational.

In a colloquy with Rep. Rhodes of Arizona, Buchanan made it clear that voluntary would not be prayer prescribed by the State, by the principal of the school, or by a teacher, or by any outside authority. Rep. Ghallagher of New Jersey still saw a problem. "The real problem with 'voluntary' is that it requires a positive act of abstention by the child, while providing a moment of silent prayer or meditation at the start of each school day makes the decision solely internal; . . ." He wanted Buchanan to accept the change to moment of silent prayer. He did not.

Rep. Drinan saw the Buchanan move as "more insidious than the original proposal." He went on,

> This amendment deletes "nondenominational." "Voluntary" is substituted for it. But "voluntary" is not the opposition of "denominational." We must assume, therefore, that every sectarian prayer or meditation and prayer, which are not really different, is now authorized under this amendment. There is much more reason to oppose the amendment than the original proposal.[20]

Rep. Buchanan was clearly supportive of the position espoused by Rep. Wylie. Buchanan stated, "This is and must be a nation under God. . . . It is our position in the people's branch of the Government to come down firmly in support of this Nation under god, not against God. . . ." Later he closed the debate with these words, "I make and rest my case on the ground that religious liberty has been denied in the public schools in America in our time. . . . The most precious liberty and right of all is being violated. Let us announce to the Nation and to history that the free exercise clause of the first amendment to the Constitution is here restored and the religious liberty of the people declared inviolate, both now and forever, so help us God." Obviously the Wylie forces hoped that through the Buchanan amendment it might be possible to accomplish their goal of slapping the Supreme Court and overturning *Engel* and *Schempp.* It was a "stealth" revision of the original proposal.[21]

Rep. Gerald Ford supported the Wylie amendment because "the Supreme Court erred in its interpretation of the First Amendment as it applies to prayer in school. The Congress has a constitutional responsibility to give the people an opportunity to decide this specific issue, and the proposed amendment deserves approval on its merits." As the debate drew to a close Mr. Richard Poff of Virginia spoke for many of his colleagues when he said, "If the amendment to delete the word 'nondenominational' and substitute the word 'voluntary' is adopted, I shall vote for the resolution."[22] The Buchanan amendment was agreed to by voice vote. On the vote on the main motion as amended the division was 240 yeas, 163 nays, 27 not voting.

Some perhaps useless math tells us that to pass the amendment required 288 votes. The sponsors were 46 shy of that number. Nineteen members who had supported the discharge petition voted against the motion. They were joined by all members who had opposed the discharge. Had Wylie retained all of those nineteen the vote for the amendment would have risen to 259. Even were all the nonvoting members added to the Wylie amendment, it still would have failed by 2 votes.

The Presidency in the 1960s and 1970s

Whenever one considers religion and the presidency in the second half of the twentieth century Billy Graham's name surfaces. In the year 1993, there he was giving both invocation and benediction at the Clinton inauguration. As we have noted, it was forty-one years earlier, with the election of Dwight Eisenhower in 1952, that the stage was set for Graham. Quickly he gained access to the White House and the power elite of the decade. While Ike often appeared more comfortable with the less strident Norman Vincent Peale, on the foreign policy front the evangelist was a natural ally in the frantic anticommunism of the 1950s. Bringing to the new, massive television audiences an Armageddon theology and a general rejection of the social gospel, Graham warned of national disaster unless the population turned to God. Graham's broadcasts became monthly warnings of imminent destruction. If the nation failed Graham's litmus test, it was doomed to see red. With a clearcut nationalistic theology Graham painted his detractors as leaning to the left. Graham lacked a political agenda apart from support for the policies of John Foster Dulles. Further, Graham seemed to sense that his own biblical literalism was unacceptable to the majority of citizens. Hence, he appeared to be preaching two gospels, biblicism for the anointed faithful, a mild civic piety for the majority. As the Eisenhower years came to a close two politicians had their eyes on the television evangelist—Richard Nixon and Lyndon Johnson.

The election of John Kennedy was not good news for Graham. Most historians view JFK as thoroughly committed to separation of church and state as Justice Black and his colleagues were defining it after 1947. Ted Sorenson observed that the president cared "not a whit for theology." He wore his religion lightly. There was no doubt about his loyalty to the Catholic Church, but he seemed to speak for a growing number in seeing faith as personal. And he certainly did not submit to ecclesiastical arm twisting, Protestant or Catholic. He was a secular president in the tradition of FDR. Kennedy was bound by doctrine in neither religion nor politics. In 1961, at his first prayer breakfast, he said, "I do not regard religion as a weapon in the Cold War."[23] One biographer observed that Kennedy cringed at hearing that Graham wished to see him. They had nothing in common. Intellectually curious, JFK's strength, his humanism, had its roots in history and ideas. Religion may have been a wellspring for him, but it certainly was no flag to be waved in a moral war.

Graham's resurrection came at the hand of Lee Harvey Oswald. Charged with enthusiasm through his public friendship with Lyndon Johnson, Graham once again coursed through the land in the cause of Johnson's foreign policy. As Vietnam replaced the Great Society in LBJ's attention, Graham's support became an ideological resource. Johnson himself carried his Vietnam crusade to the country in the guise of a religious revival. In the fall of 1967 LBJ employed old Bruton Parish Church in Williamsburg, Virginia, the legendary church of Washington, Mason, and Henry, to close his speaking tour on behalf of Vietnam policy. As fate would have it a minister not known for leadership or controversy used his sermon to challenge Johnson's policies in a telling engagement between "mitre and sceptre." The rector was widely criticized for "abuse" of the pulpit. Few suggested LBJ had abused the pew. Johnson's religious crusade faltered and

1968 brought an end to his political career. Now Graham had his second friend on tap.

Unlike LBJ, Hubert Humphrey had no place for Graham as a spiritual advisor. Humphrey was far more theologically literate than the preacher. A civil rights advocate, he was motivated by a serious examination of the social message of the prophet Amos. Humphrey was certainly not an option for Graham.

Some observers, in the summer of 1968, said that Graham had personally persuaded Richard Nixon to run for president. At least Graham was at the center of Nixon's entourage. And whether or not the evangelist had any effect on Nixon's decision to run, it is clear that once in the fray Graham unapologetically cast him his support. In what came to be a very close election, that support may well have been decisive.

When Quaker Nixon took office in 1969 he moved quickly to establish what Reinhold Niebuhr described as the "King's Chapel in the King's Court." The president inaugurated a "by invitation only" religious service in the White House for his administrative family. It was an idea Graham had first advanced to Lady Bird Johnson the previous year. Nixon said its purpose was furthering the cause of religion. It did far more, coopting a portion of the religious community in the support of government policy. Toward the end of his presidency Nixon used the White House Sunday gathering, at which prominent and acceptable clergy were invited to preach, as a means of discipline. When Secretary Hickel publicly disagreed with Nixon over student protests he was pointedly told he was not welcome at the service.

Preoccupied with Vietnam and then Watergate, Nixon had little time for any incipient fundamentalist political agenda. As for Graham, apart from his support for Becker's and Dirksen's public school prayer amendments, he had no organized political agenda. Nixon favored prayer in schools but, as we have noticed, neither he nor his administration played a significant role in the 1971 House debates.

By 1973 the Nixon presidency was in serious trouble. Little attention was directed to the landmark *Roe* v. *Wade* decision by the Supreme Court. While Jerry Falwell became galvanized to political action by that Court opinion, White House religion was otherwise engaged. When Nixon, who had made religion so visibly a part of the first family, left office in disgrace, morally bankrupt, Graham's star declined.

Gerald Ford presented a quite different style to the public, one that included a quiet religious sentiment that found no reason for flamboyant religious mentors. President Jimmy Carter likewise saw religion in personal terms. He is a man of intense religious conviction quite comfortable discussing that faith on his own terms in the secular arena. Americans became familiar, many for the first time, with the phrase "born again." It signified for Carter no dogmatic narrowness but rather a personal experience of faith. Some feared that his openness to religious conversation would mean a collapse of support for the Supreme Court's church/state decisions. This fear was fueled by the presence of a new chief justice, Warren Burger, as well as other Nixon- and Ford-appointed colleagues. However, the Burger era showed little inclination to move from the Warren Court foundations in church/state matters.

Carter demonstrated a vigorous commitment to religious freedom that embraced the Madisonian tradition. Like Jefferson and other founders, Carter recognized religion as private and personal. Religious dogma and doctrine should not be a part of public policy. Carter practiced his religion with fervor while guarding with tenacity the constitutional principle of free exercise. His administration gave the lie to all those who argue that recent Supreme Court decisions preclude persons of faith from public service.

Predictably, this born again Southern Baptist became the target of reactionary fundamentalists as they emerged in the cable television era to become politically active. Carter's faith did not satisfy them because they believed religion should be written into law. Carter, it was argued, had betrayed the religious community with his support for the Equal Rights Amendment and federal funding for abortion clinics. Interestingly, fundamentalists used the very same tactics as those they suggested John Kennedy would use were he elected in 1960. As Carter's term came to a close another wave of prayer amendments was on the way, now reinvigorated by a politicized religious right.

Notes

1. *Congressional Record*, Vol. 117, Part 30, November 2, 1971, to November 8, 1971 (Washington, D.C.: United States Government Printing Office, 1971), p. 39890. On the same theme, Rep. Drinan noted,

> There is one overwhelming reason why some Members of this House feel that they must vote for the Wylie amendment today. That reason is fear of the political consequences of a vote which opponents in a forthcoming election could allege to be a vote against God, against piety and against morality. . . . One Member told me categorically that he expects to vote for the Wylie amendment because he does not want to bother explaining to constituents and others for the next several months why he voted "against prayer." (CR, p. 39899)

2. *Congressional Record*, p. 39892.
3. Ibid., p. 39895.
4. Ibid., p. 39886.
5. Ibid., p. 39896.
6. The record of the debate consumed over seventy pages of the

Congressional Record. Members continually mixed the Wylie and Buchanan amendments. It is of interest that Rep. Buchanan, despite his views on the prayer amendment, was targeted for defeat in Alabama by religious right forces. The republican congressman was beaten. In the eighties he became chairman of People for the American Way.

7. Ibid., p. 38694.

8. U.S. Congress, Senate, Hearings before the Subcommittee on Constitutional Amendments, *School Prayers* (Washington, D.C.: U.S. Government Printing Office, 1966), p. 86.

9. *Congressional Record*, p. 39898.

10. Ibid., p. 39909.

11. Ibid., p. 39910.

12. Ibid., p. 39916. Former Rep. Becker was in the House for this part of the debate.

13. Ibid.

14. "The astounding thing about this text is that it addresses itself only by indirection, if at all, to the problem which actually interests its sponsors, and which actually concerned the Supreme Court in the cases it is designed to overrule or weaken—the problem of official prayer in the public schools. The question in the school prayer cases was not whether people might sometimes lawfully pray in buildings supported in whole or in part by public funds. The question was whether children, not so much 'lawfully assembled' in public buildings as coerced into assembling in public buildings by the truancy laws, could lawfully be forced either to pray, or to stand silent during a prayer conducted in their coerced presence, or to be sent into the hall or in some other way marked as deviants, with all that means to a child. Of this proposed amendment as it stands, therefore, one of two things must be true. Either it does not touch the practice of school prayer at all (in which case it is a triviality, addressing itself to peripheral problems which interest no one) or it will be held to overrule the school prayer cases, without doing so in candid language that addresses itself fairly to the problem of official coercion, or shaming, operating upon children in connection with religious matters. If the first of these things is true,

then it is preposterous to go through the constitutional amendment process to achieve so trivial a result. If the second should turn out to be true, then a real outrage will have been committed, because a coercion of children in religious concerns, or a pressure upon them in regard to such concerns, will turn out to have been made permissible, by language which does not in any way make clear this drastic purpose." (*Congressional Record*, pp. 39922-23)

15. *Congressional Record*, p. 39929.

16. Ibid., p. 39931.

17. Ibid., p. 39940.

18. Ibid., p. 39947.

19. Ibid., p. 39948.

20. Ibid., pp. 39950-51.

21. Ibid., pp. 39946, 39957.

22. Ibid., p. 39956.

23. *Public Papers of the President of the United States: John F. Kennedy—1961* (Washington, D.C.: U.S. Government Printing Office, 1962), p. 77.

11

The Reagan/Bush Years:
Republican Senate, Renewed Struggle

As the election year 1980 approached, a new direction was adopted by some opponents of the Supreme Court's prayer decisions. In 1979 Sen. Jesse Helms of North Carolina introduced a legislative rider that would have forbidden the Supreme Court to review any case concerning voluntary prayer in the public schools. The first hearings on that subject took place in the House in July, August, and September 1980.

House Hearings, 1980

The House Committee on the Judiciary's Subcommittee on Courts, Civil Liberties, and the Administration of Justice convened on July 29, 1980, under the chairmanship of Robert Kastenmeier of Wisconsin. In his opening remarks Kastenmeier reviewed the history of Court activity regarding school prayer before laying out the following background for the current inquiry.

A serious attempt in 1971 to amend the Constitution to overturn this view [*Engel* and *Schempp*] failed in Congress and now, in 1980, we are faced with a new challenge to the integrity of the first amendment. Senator Jesse Helms has authored an amendment to a minor judicial reform bill which would have the effect of eliminating the authority of the Supreme Court and other Federal courts to make rulings regarding the constitutionality of any State laws or regulations which relate to prayer in public schools or buildings.

This amendment was agreed to by the Senate[1] as part of a legislative compromise designed to save the legislation creating the Department of Education. This legislation raises several serious constitutional and policy questions which I hope we can focus on during these hearings.

First, the Helms amendment could well pave the way for some State courts to try to overturn the Supreme Court's clear judgment that the Government has no business in religion. Conceivably this could result in 50 interpretations of the meaning of the first amendment. It must be determined if this would square with the strong public interest in developing and maintaining clear, definitive, and nationwide resolutions of issues of constitutional dimension.

Second, the Helms amendment would for the first time remove the authority of the Supreme Court to decide a controversy of a constitutional nature. There is serious doubt as to whether this statutory procedure would itself be constitutional.[2]

The heart of the Helms proposal, S. 450, as far as these hearings were concerned was the following language:

The Supreme Court shall not have jurisdiction to review, by appeal, writ of certiorari, or otherwise, any case arising out of any State statute, ordinance, rule, regulation, or any part thereof, or arising out of any Act interpreting, applying, or enforcing a State statute, ordinance, rule, or regulation, which relates to voluntary prayers in public schools and public buildings.[3]

Rep. Tom Railsback of Illinois was the first to speak after the chair's opening comments. He raised questions about the right of Congress to restrict the Court as suggested, but then added:

> Prayer in the public schools is said to be the desire of an overwhelming majority of the American people. I do not question that statistic. But we are not talking here about the rights of majorities. Rather we are talking about the rights of one person. That is what the first amendment is all about. That is what the Bill of Rights is all about. To protect an individual against the coercive power of Government, to protect the unpopular minority from the will of the majority.[4]

At that point the full weight of the Carter administration came into play as John Harmon, assistant attorney general in the Justice Department, reaffirmed a position taken by the department in a letter of June 19, 1980, to Rep. Peter Rodino of New Jersey, chair of the Judiciary Committee. "As the attached opinion from the Office of Legal Counsel makes clear, we believe that the 'Helms amendment' is unconstitutional to the extent that it would purport to divest the Supreme Court of its jurisdiction to hear this class of controversies."[5] The letter continued by expressing "vigorous opposition to the 'Helms amendment.'"

Although the focus had been shifted from constitutional amendment to legislation designed to limit the Supreme Court's jurisdiction, many of the same persons appeared to testify. The National Council of Churches, most main stream denominations, most Jewish organizations, the Parent-Teacher Association, and the American Civil Liberties Union vigorously opposed the Helms amendment. In support were the Orthodox rabbis, the National Association of Evangelicals, and the American Legion. New to the stage was the Christian right, represented by Campus Crusade director Bill Bright, television preacher and evangelist James Robison, and Robert Billings for Moral Majority.

Bill Bright, seeing no inherent contradiction in his assertions, said he would "defend voluntary prayer. And again, the most important thing is that we, a nation born with faith, under faith in God, dedicated to Jesus Christ from our very founding, would once again recognize, in fact, that we do believe in God and we do acknowledge our heritage."[6] Bright introduced extreme fundamentalist interpretations of the Bible to make his case. In taking that approach he was in marked contrast with the presentations in past years by the National Association of Evangelicals.[7] Bright saw the Supreme Court decisions as the "rejection of the Lord from the public schools which had been born in the cradle of the church." He asked the committee to consider the plagues that followed the decisions.

> Within a short time, President Kennedy had been assassinated. It would be easy to say, "Well, that would have happened anyway." The Vietnam War began to accelerate, and it was only a couple of years before the Gulf of Tonkin Resolution and the massive American build-up in Southeast Asia. . . . The drug culture began to escalate rapidly. Crime accelerated. American families began disintegrating. . . . Racial conflict in cities turned bloody and whole blocks were burned. . . . Senator Robert Kennedy was assassinated, then Dr. Martin Luther King. . . .[8]

The Moral Majority, in the person of Professor Charles Rice of the Notre Dame University Law School, presented a far more reasoned argument for the Helms amendment. The committee did elicit the admission from Rice that the Helms provision goes so far "as banning the Bill of Rights or first amendment cases from the Supreme Court."[9]

The subject of voluntary prayer was frequently raised as definitions were sought. Professor Thomas Emerson of the Yale Law School, speaking on behalf of the American Civil Liberties Union, made the following suggestion.

> The attempt to make the religious observance seem to be voluntary takes either of two forms. Either allowing the sermon to be performed by others or to be arranged by others or allowing pupils to be exempt from the sermon. Neither course of action solves the problem. Exclusion does not eliminate the pressure to conform and so an organization by children is inconceivable. So arrangements would have to be made by religious leaders in the community and that would simply compound the difficulty. In any event the sermon still takes place in the school under auspices of school officials and in the context of a public institution.[10]

The hearings concluded two months before the presidential election. The result of the House consideration was defeat for the Helms amendment in spite of passage by the Senate in 1979. A new, Republican Senate Judiciary Committee in 1981 would bring together a panel of constitutional experts to discuss the Helms proposal. The appearance of the Moral Majority was a sign of a new political force that would help elect a Republican Senate majority and place Sen. Strom Thurmond in the chair of the Senate Judiciary Committee for six years.[11]

Reagan and the Religious Right

The election of 1980 did not center upon prayer in schools but it was a primary concern for the newly minted Moral Majority that, under the leadership of Jerry Falwell, Howard Phillips, Richard Viguerie, Ed McAteer, and Paul Weyrich, unabashedly endorsed Ronald Reagan's candidacy. *Newsweek* featured Falwell on its September 15 cover with the headline "Born-Again Politics." It was, a far cry from the use of that term just four years earlier by Jimmy Carter.

In the first week in October the regional convention of the National Religious Broadcasters met in Lynchburg, Virginia, with the theme "One nation . . . under God . . . Indivisible." For anyone who watched the participants in that meeting it was clear that a new sense of self-esteem had invigorated this group of fundamentalists, in the past so frequently dismissed by mainstream Protestants as an irrelevant and pathetic fringe group. Billy Graham had achieved acceptance in the mainstream by identifying his revivals with the established churches. That fall in Lynchburg there may have been admiration for Graham by the assembled broadcasters, but he was not part of their world.

The convention heard Falwell at lunch affirm that Jews could not pray to God unless they accepted Jesus Christ.[12] After lunch the group moved to the Liberty Baptist College campus for the making of resolutions, prior to the arrival of the honored guest, Ronald Reagan. Even as the broadcasters concluded that they could not officially endorse Reagan without endangering their FCC licenses, Falwell operatives distributed bumper stickers emblazoned with "Christians for Reagan."

Reagan's attachment to the religious right seems to have blossomed in his years as governor of California. In his biography of Reagan, written with the cooperation of the White House, Bob

Slosser claims to have been at Reagan's home in 1970 when George Otis recounted a vision to his host. "If you walk uprightly before me you will reside at 1600 Pennsylvania Avenue." The governor's single word response—"Well!"[13]

The religious right, seeking to translate private ideology into public virtue, found a candidate who would deliver on that score even if his church attendance was "spotty." There is little evidence to suggest that Reagan either understood or shared the biblicism espoused by the Moral Majority, but he was an eager player in their political game. Reagan's election was hailed as an act of the deity by many from the fundamentalist camp. By that time Pat Robertson had severed his ties with the Moral Majority and was making his own deals with the White House.

One of the targets for conquest in the minds of the fundamentalists was the Southern Baptist Convention, the largest Protestant denomination in the country. On June 13, 1982, Vice President Bush, an Episcopalian, addressed thousands of messengers to the annual Southern Baptist Convention meeting in New Orleans. He urged that body to abandon generations of support for separation of church and state and cast their lot with Reagan's school prayer amendment.[14] Morton Blackwell, special assistant to Reagan, urged his friend Ed McAteer, a Southern Baptist, to create a convention resolution endorsing the prayer amendment so that the messengers could follow the Bush advice. It was done and endorsed.[15] Three years later pastors of that same convention, assembled for the purpose of purging heretics from the denomination, were praised by Reagan. He stated his "agreement with the spiritual values of the group."[16] Of course it would be foolish to assume that President Reagan had a clue as to what Southern Baptists were about in the 1980s.

One of the strangest events of Reagan's presidency took place in 1983 when, having met with leaders of the religious right,

Reagan delivered himself of the following astounding assertion: "I turn back to your ancient prophets in the Old Testament and the signs foretelling Armageddon, and I find myself wondering if—if we're the generation that is going to see that come about."[17] This was at a time when both Pat Robertson and Falwell were predicting the end of the world prior to the year 2000. Such philosophy shoots the hell out of strategic planning and budget restraints, not to mention national defense. Little wonder that the newly configured Senate took up the subject of school prayer in the spring of 1981.

Senate Hearings on Restraining the Judiciary, 1981

On May 20, 1981, the Subcommittee on the Constitution of the Senate Judiciary Committee commenced hearings on "Constitutional Restraints Upon the Judiciary." The chair of the full committee was Sen. Strom Thurmond. The subcommittee was chaired by Sen. Orrin Hatch of Utah. Serving with him on the committee were Thurmond, Charles Grassley of Iowa, Dennis DeConcini of Arizona, and Patrick Leahy of Vermont. Sen. DeConcini had supported the Helms amendment, passed in the Senate in 1979.

The purpose of the proposals before the committee had much to do with school prayer but they addressed specific constitutional questions of congressional authority. Early on Sen. Leahy attempted to define the limits of the hearing.

> There are really two distinct areas for us to examine in these hearings, and both are vital. The first is the extent of Congress' authority under Article III of the Constitution to control the jurisdiction of both the lower Federal courts and the Supreme Court. The second area is the question of how and to what

extent the Congress ought to exercise its constitutional authority, however broad or narrow it is, to alter the existing
jurisdiction of either the lower Federal courts or all Federal
courts.[18]

The issue had been addressed by the House committee in 1980
largely through the testimony of religious representatives. That
committee focused on the purpose of the legislation. The Senate
chose to limit itself primarily to procedures. In order to accomplish
that the Senate Committee invited only constitutional experts,
twelve prominent scholars of constitutional law. Of the 867 pages
of material, only 105 pages were devoted to oral testimony and
questions. The purpose was clearly to amass a scholarly treatise
for study and digestion. Thus, while the bills before the Congress
involved primarily school prayer, and to a lesser extent school
busing and abortion, little time was devoted to those problems
as such.

The constitutional clause at issue was the following:

Art. III, #2. In all Cases affecting Ambassadors, other public
Ministers and Consuls, and those in which a State shall be
a Party, the supreme Court shall have original Jurisdiction. In
all other Cases before mentioned, the supreme Court shall have
appellate Jurisdiction, both as to Law and Fact, with such
Exceptions and under such Regulations as the Congress shall
make.

Since the Constitution authorized the Congress to create such
lower courts as it deemed wise and necessary, there was little
question as to the power of Congress to control them. Professor
William Van Alstyne argued, "The clause does not know any
interior restrictions. The emphasis is appropriately on the adjec-

tive 'such.' That is to say, such exceptions as Congress shall make."[19] A number of other scholars agreed.

On the other side Professor Telford Taylor contended, "I know nothing in constitutional history which would support the idea that Congressional power over court jurisdiction was intended as a means by which Congress may foreclose or nullify Supreme Court decisions construing and enforcing constitutional limitations. So applied, the power over jurisdiction would leave the legislative branch bound only by its own interpretation of its own powers, and would move this nation a long way towards the English system of Parliamentary supremacy."[20]

When it came to Leahy's second question, the experts were in general agreement that it would be unwise and dangerous to exercise the power if, indeed, the Congress had the power. Professor Paul Bator wrote, "And finally, such a measure would create a host of serious and perhaps intolerable problems in the fair and rational administration of the laws." However, Professor Charles Rice, who had testified in 1980 before the House committee on behalf of the Moral Majority, felt it was appropriate for the Congress to exercise the power it possessed.

Finally, on September 24, 1982, the Senate killed the Helms proposal, which had by then been attached to a debt-ceiling bill. A filibuster that lasted a month and involved several senators proved successful when cloture failed on seven occasions, the last by a vote of fifty-three to forty-five.[21] It would have taken sixty votes to cut off debate. Sen. Helms finally moved to recommit the debt-ceiling measure to committee with instructions to report back a clean bill with his prayer amendment included, but this motion was tabled by a vote of fifty-one to forty-eight.[22]

Senate Hearings, 1982

Meanwhile, President Reagan, true to his promise, submitted a proposed constitutional prayer amendment, S.J. Res. 199, to the Senate on May 17, 1982. It read, "Nothing in this Constitution shall be construed to prohibit individual or group prayer in public schools or other public institutions. No person shall be required by the United States or by any State to participate in prayer."[23] Hearings on this latest edition began before the full Committee of the Judiciary on July 29, 1982. Two other days of hearings were held, one in August, the last on September 16, eight days before the Helms rider was defeated on the floor.

Chairman Thurmond, a genuine prayer amendment advocate, set the tone for the sessions with his opening remarks.

> President Reagan has, in my view, correctly and courageously acknowledged what is recognized to be a vital part of our American Government.
>
> The evidence that we are a religious people surrounds us— in our coinage, in our national anthem, in our pledge of allegiance. As President pro tempore of the Senate, I have the privilege of opening the Senate each day that it is in session. My first act after calling the Senate to order is to recognize the Chaplain of the Senate, who offers our opening prayer. . . . Our Nation is founded on that premise (In God We Trust) and our faith in God, expressed through prayer, is richly ingrained in American history. Now, public opinion favors voluntary prayer. The American people are openly and overwhelmingly in favor of allowing prayer in our public schools.[24]

Turning to his long-held states rights agenda, so vigorously pursued by him in an effort to prevent integration in his native South and his native state, South Carolina, in the 1950s and

1960s, Thurmond began an attack on the Supreme Court's usurpation of "the constitutional authority of the States over church-state relations. . . . The 14th amendment was not intended to be used to change the meaning of the establishment clause." As to the intention of the First Amendment, Thurmond insisted that its language "was intended to prevent any national ecclesiastical establishment and leave each State free to define the meaning of religious establishment under its own constitution and laws."

On the question of a "national" church, that term was, as we have noted earlier, never intended to endorse a plural establishment, which Madison feared more than a single one. As to original intent, Thurmond was quite correct that in 1789 the Congress extended the reach of the amendment only to the federal government. But his quarrel should have been with the Confederate troops who lost the Civil War in 1865, thereby securing a more perfect union. The Fourteenth Amendment was made necessary because of the enslavement of human beings in the South. And its reach, as later Supreme Court justices determined, included the Bill of Rights. That, of course, was Madison's wish from the beginning.

Thurmond's argument that the Reagan amendment "would reinstate . . . the original intent of the Founding Fathers," followed by the notion that it "permits individual and group prayer in public schools"[25] fails to note that there were no public schools in 1792 and that nothing the Court had decided precluded individual and group prayers in schools today.

For the first time since the issue arose for national debate in 1962, the Republicans were in control of the committee that would address a constitutional amendment about prayer. However, the first Senate committee hearing in 1962, under the Democrats, was far more biased, inviting only critics of *Engel* to testify. One felt at the time that the year 1982 was the critical moment for proponents of a prayer amendment. With the full prestige of the White House finally behind them and a Republican Senate eager to make a mark in this area, it was the best of times to achieve their goal.

The first witness was Sen. Mark Hatfield of Oregon, who injected a new note into the deliberations. He had no problem with the *Engel* decision concerning "a routine, formalistic, and spiritually bankrupt prayer." What concerned him was "access" to places of meeting for young persons who wished to pray or meditate in school rooms before and after class hours. He and several colleagues had fashioned an Equal Access Bill that would, in 1984, pass overwhelmingly both in the House (337 to 77) and in the Senate (88 to 11). It was designed to extend the application of the *Widmar* decision to public schools. In 1990 the 1984 act was upheld in the *Mergens* case.[26]

An early parade of witnesses favoring the Reagan amendment included Sen. Helms, whose chief scholarly witness was James McClellan,[27] who had written an essay for a foundation headed by Paul Weyrich, aided by a vice president for operations, Robert Billings, a White House advisor. Early in the session a letter from President Reagan was read. It argued, "The amendment will allow communities to determine for themselves whether prayer should be permitted in their public schools and to allow individuals to decide for themselves whether they wish to participate in prayer."[28] The Justice Department spoke for the administration and its justification for the amendment included this description of a type of prayer.

If school authorities choose to lead a group prayer, the selection of the particular prayer—subject of course to the right of those not wishing to participate not to do so—would be left to the judgment of local communities, based on a consideration of such factors as the desires of parents, students and teachers and other community interests consistent with applicable state law. The amendment does not limit the types of prayer that are constitutionally permissible and is not intended to afford a basis for intervention by federal courts to determine whether or not particular prayers are appropriate for individuals or groups to recite.[29]

Interestingly, the Reagan entourage made much of the fact that they believed, erroneously I have argued earlier, that Congress only meant to exclude a single religion as established at the national level. Yet this assignment to the community of the power to prescribe a prayer consistent with local majority opinion was merely a national religion writ small.

The next panel of witnesses included Ed McAteer of the Christian Roundtable. He was followed by a group representing the National Council of Churches, Jewish communities, Southern Baptists, and Lutherans. Dean Kelley of the National Council of Churches addressed the amendment with the following comment, "Now that, in our view, is an abandonment of the heroic experiment of the first amendment. It is a clear regression to territorialism because what is happening there is that a religious form becomes the dominant one, usually that of the majority— which is the 'prince,' the ruler in our society."[30]

There were few other significant moments in a hearing that was rapidly declining into a dialogue between a couple of senators and those testifying. In fact, on the final day only Sen. Arlen Specter of Pennsylvania attended. The U.S. attorney general's office sent two deputies and after a rather extended discussion with Specter, one of them said he expected the amendment to pass, "We believe that they will devise ways in which those who do not agree with the expression reflected in the prayer, or who are members of a religious minority in that particular community, will feel comfortable in not participating."[31] Again, the discussion turned on the word voluntary.

Pat Robertson put in an appearance in which he informed the committee that his father, A. Willis Robertson, a former senator from Virginia, "met every Wednesday with colleagues to pray in the Senate dining room—and to him that was the highlight of his week."[32] With only Specter present a distinguished panel of constitutional law professors offered a significant moment in the three-day process. William Van Alstyne of Duke University said, "There usually does emerge one witness whose merely extemporaneous remarks are so special that they quite justly dominate the proceedings. I think we have heard those remarks quite frankly."[33] He was referring to the testimony of Professor Norman Redlich of New York University Law School. Those comments are printed in appendix C.

Following the hearings there was no legislative action taken by either house of Congress for the remainder of the year. But after the November 1982 election, the Congress returned to face another round of hearings on the prayer amendment.

Senate Hearings, 1983

On March 24, 1983, Sens. Thurmond and Hatch reintroduced S.J. Res. 199 (see page 197) under the new label S.J. Res. 73. Two days of hearings, on April 29 and May 2, by the Judiciary Subcommittee on the Constitution resulted in a reporting of S.J. Res. 73 to the full committee along with a new amendment, S.J. Res. 212, offered by Sens. Thurmond, Hatch, and Grassley. On June 27 the full Judiciary Committee held a day of hearings. In addition, the committee held two days of hearings solely on equal access, addressed by section 2 of S.J. Res. 212.

A brief review of the three days of hearings in 1983 reveals a continued parade of voices similar to those raised in other years. There was an obvious movement toward some form of silent meditation language and a growing willingness to dispense with the term "prayer." Following the hearings, S.J. Res. 73, which was identical to Reagan's proposal of 1982, was amended with the addition of the words, "Neither the United States nor any State shall compose the words of any prayer to be said in public schools."[34]

There were a few important moments in the 1983 hearings. It was evident in his opening remarks that Hatch was not altogether satisfied with the language of S.J. Res. 73. "I am also concerned about how the content of any group prayer is to be determined."

The problems of prayer content and source became a major theme as witness after witness raised questions about even the most circumscribing language on the subjects.

One of the more striking dilemmas in this debate was the public perception of Supreme Court decisions that appeared to trigger many extreme actions by school administrators in order to avoid prosecution for constitutional violations. Professor Walter Dellinger of Duke University placed his finger adroitly on the problem.

Senator, our problem is this: the Supreme Court's decisions have only invalidated teacher-led, school-initiated, government-sponsored prayer. Now this committee has heard accurate statements from around the country that there are school principals who say, "We cannot allow the Fellowship of Christian Athletes to have a meeting at our school, even though we permit the key club and the rodeo club to meet." There are school principals around the country who think that. Do you know why they think that? They think that, in part, because the President of the United States and many distinguished Members of Congress have for many years been misleading the American people by constantly stating that the U.S. Supreme Court has forbidden all prayer in the public schools. That is just not true.

Even though there were separate hearings held that year on equal access, the subject continued to surface in exchanges during the three days of this hearing. Senator Hatch asked a spokesman for the Justice Department whether he felt a constitutional amendment was necessary to deal with equal access. Mr. Schmults replied in the affirmative. Aware of that Professor Dellinger addressed the issue with a quite accurate prediction. The Supreme Court had decided in the *Widmar* case that equal access at the college level was required under the First Amendment. In that case there was a footnote, "We do not reach in this case the high school issue." Dellinger commented, "I am willing to bet the mortgage that in a case involving truly student-initiated, voluntary prayer activities in a public setting, the Supreme Court will apply the principles of *Widmar* and forbid discrimination against extracurricular activities involving religious speech."[35] Of course he was proved correct in the *Mergens* case of 1990.

As the hours passed the evidence mounted that experts on both sides of the divide on the efficacy of school prayer were concluding, as did Professor Burke Marshall of Yale, that "the core objection to the resolution is that it inescapably leaves the matter of the choice of the prayer or prayers to be offered as part of a school program up to the agents of the state."[36] Nevertheless, the Moral Majority remained convinced that prescribed prayer presented no problems because "local school districts have rarely ever sought to stifle diversity or to offend those who hold minority religious views."[37]

Sensitive to the growing sentiment against the Reagan amendment, Hatch unveiled his new amendment, S.J. Res. 212:

Section 1. Nothing in this Constitution shall be construed to prohibit individual or group silent prayer or meditation in public schools. Neither the United States nor any State shall require any person to participate in such prayer or meditation, nor shall they encourage any particular form of prayer or meditation.

Section 2. Nothing in the Constitution shall be construed to prohibit equal access to the use of public school facilities by all voluntary student groups.

Hatch said it "would only permit individual or group silent prayer or meditation. It would not permit the expression of denominational prayer, or of any other oral or vocal prayer."[38]

Returning to speak to the full committee, Dellinger took the occasion to dissect the Reagan amendment. He stated that the new (S.J. Res. 212) resolution was not fundamentally inconsistent with Supreme Court opinions but S.J. Res. 73 "has a central vice which the Deputy Attorney General successfully avoids discussing, and that vice is this: It opens the way to Government control of religion. The administration avoids whenever possible discussing the critical question of who will be empowered to compose those prayers for oral group recitation in the public schools."[39] Though it would still muster considerable support on the Senate floor, the Reagan amendment was doomed.

After a meeting on July 14, 1983, at which both resolutions were amended, the committee reported them to the full Senate without recommendation. The vote was fourteen to three. On

March 20, 1984, the full Senate voted on the president's prayer amendment (S.J. Res. 73). The vote, fifty-six to forty-four, fell eleven votes short of the two-thirds required.

The vote was made possible following an arrangement between Senate Majority Leader Howard Baker of Tennessee and Sen. Lowell Weicker of Connecticut. Weicker had threatened a filibuster against the prayer amendment. He agreed to "permit a vote on the amendment—and only that one." Baker was banking on enough senators voting for the president's proposal because of the upcoming November elections. Weicker was secure that he had the votes required to defeat the amendment on the floor. He was less certain that he could have stopped an alternative silent reflection proposal that some like Sen. Alan Dixon of Illinois desired to offer. Baker miscalculated and the prayer amendment died.

The Focus Shifts: Equal Access

On March 28, 1984, a subcommittee of the House Committee on Education and Labor began hearings on the "Religious Speech Protection Act." In contrast with the approach taken by Sen. Hatch in 1983, this new proposal was to be an act of Congress, not a constitutional amendment. A new cast of characters addressed many of the same old issues with many of the same old witnesses. But alignments were changing. Dean Kelley, speaking for the National Council of Churches commented, "It grieves me to be here differing with some of the allies with whom we worked to oppose the amendment of the Constitution to permit state-mandated teacher-led prayer in public schools. But the difference, I think, is important because the National Council of Churches . . . gave approval to the concept [of equal access]." Equal access, he insisted, brought "religious speech up to scratch, on a par of equality, with other forms of speech."[40] On the other side of the issue was the American Civil Liberties Union, which found serious problems with the provision in H.R. 4996 that provided for a cutoff of federal funds to schools that failed to comply and allowed schools to permit access during the school day. Both of those provisions were removed before passage of H.R. 1310,[41] a math-science bill that contained a modified equal access rider.

Prayer and the Senate Judiciary Committee Once Again, 1984

On June 26, 1984, the Judiciary's Subcommittee on the Constitution convened for one day to hold a hearing on the topic "Issues in Religious Liberty." The obvious stimulus for this occasion was the conviction of Sun Myung Moon over charges brought by the Internal Revenue Service. It was also concerned with alleged harassment of religious groups for noncompliance with state statutes, largely in the areas of child abuse and private schooling. Strong support for Moon came from Professor Laurence Tribe of Harvard as well as from the committee chair, Sen. Hatch. There was some excessive rhetoric by James Kennedy, a minister from Florida, concerning separation of church and state. "The American Constitution does not teach separation of church and State. It is however explicitly taught in the Soviet Constitution."[42] Herbert Titus of what is now Regent University, Pat Robertson's college in Virginia Beach, weighed in against the American Civil Liberties Union and "others" for seeking to stop the proclamation of 1983 as the year of the Bible.[43] He also railed against those groups who had kept "the Bible as the Word of God not only out of the public school classroom but off public school grounds almost altogether."[44]

Senator Helms and President Reagan One More Time

On January 3, 1985, Sen. Helms made another effort to have his colleagues vote on his bill, which would

> take advantage of the congressional authority, given explicitly in Article III of the Constitution, to regulate the general juris-diction of the inferior federal courts and the appellate juris-diction of the Supreme Court. The bill [S.47] curtails such jurisdiction so that federal courts no longer have the power to hear cases involving voluntary prayer, Bible reading, and religious meetings in the public schools.[45]

Once again Helms failed to muster the necessary votes.

The valiant Republican effort to guide the president's amend-ment through the Congress continued into 1985 with the advocacy of S.J. Res. 2. Stripped of its earlier vocal prayer content, the amendment read: "Nothing in this Constitution shall be construed to prohibit individual or group silent prayer or reflection in public schools. Neither the United States nor any State shall require any person to participate in such prayer or reflection, nor shall they encourage any particular form of prayer or reflection."[46] An immediate response might have been that the proponents had accepted the application of the First Amendment to the states resulting from passage of the Fourteenth Amendment. How else would one explain the prohibition applied to state legislation? This proved significant since much of the testimony on amend-ments since 1962 had been focused upon what was argued to be a misreading by the Supreme Court of the intention of the Fourteenth Amendment.

The timing of the Senate hearing was fortuitous or disastrous, depending upon the point of view. On June 4, fifteen days before the hearing began, the Supreme Court handed down its decision in *Wallace* v. *Jaffree*. By a six-to-three margin the justices, in an opinion written by Justice John Paul Stevens, overturned an Alabama law establishing a moment of silence in the state's public schools. On its face, the ruling would appear to have given impetus to proponents of the Reagan amendment. But upon examination of the arguments it became clear that the Court finding was focused on the purpose of the Alabama law. The Court found a legislative intent "to return prayer to the public schools." It was the same argument the Court had used in 1980 in *Stone* v. *Graham*, when it declared unconstitutional a Kentucky law requiring the posting of the Ten Commandments in public schoolrooms. Further, in a concurring opinion Justice Sandra Day O'Connor left open the possibility that a more carefully worded moment-of-silence law might well pass muster. Justice Lewis Powell agreed with her on that point. Taking those two justices plus the three dissenters, there was a majority of the Court prepared to accept in state legislation some form of silent moment in public classrooms. Sen. Specter made that point in his opening remarks to the committee, in which he opposed S.J. Res. 2.

The movement in the testimony away from vocal prayer was evidenced in the remarks of Michael Malbin of the American Enterprise Institute. "I believe without reservation that a national vocal prayer amendment, no matter how qualified, would be dangerous, far worse than the status quo after *Jaffree*, and I say this despite all the criticisms that you know I have made of all the Court's rules of law since *Everson*."[47] Malbin favored the amendment before the committee, but only because it rejected vocal or oral prayer. In that moment the enthusiasm for the newly defined cause had to be diminished. This could be felt in the scorching testimony of Thomas Parker, attorney for Alabama in the *Jaffree* case. He felt the Court was asserting that "any mention of God or Christ is viewed as challenging the very deification of man and reason under secular humanism."[48] Further, he felt that the justices had violated their oaths and should be impeached. He thus made it clear that the Court had properly read the intent of the Alabama law.

Dean Kelley, speaking for the National Council of Churches, properly observed, "We think the proposed amendments are unnecessary, since any person can pray to God at any time or place. The Supreme Court cannot prevent it, and has not attempted to, and the Congress cannot enable it." His words were a clear signal that the religious fundamentalists would find the new version of an amendment almost useless to their cause—state support for deity.

Sen. Thurmond could read the political winds and although he preferred allowing "voluntary vocal prayer," he was prepared to support the new wording "if we do not have support for voluntary prayer."[49] More clearly than before the testimony was on the record that what proponents meant by voluntary prayer was organized prayer from which one could absent oneself. Jerry Falwell's slogan "Kids Need to Pray" was seen for what it always had been, a plea for sectarian affirmations about deity that presumably matched the majority opinion in localities across the country.

The president's amendment went down to defeat and with the change to a Democratic majority in the Senate in 1987 the leadership of the Judiciary Committee passed to Sen. Joseph Biden of Delaware who found no reason to continue the hearing marathon of the past five years. Further, with the Supreme Court nominations of Robert Bork, Anthony Kennedy, David Souter, and Clarence Thomas successively appearing on the agenda, there was little time to explore church/state issues. And the strategy of those who most vigorously questioned the nominees included the intentional omission of questions on church/state matters. Sen. Specter supplied the most frequent inquiries about relevant cases in that area, most of them reflecting a serious commitment to separation.

Sporadic efforts to revive the prayer question surfaced from time to time. On January 23, 1992, Sen. Helms sought to amend the Neighborhood Schools Improvement Act to express a "sense of the Senate" that the Supreme Court should use the *Lee v. Weisman* case to reverse *Engel* and *Schempp*. In his argument for the rider he insisted that the deterioration of school discipline began with those decisions. Helms said he offered the proposal so that voluntary prayer and Bible reading could be returned to public schools. During a two-hour debate Sen. Helms suffered a major blow to his efforts when Sen. Thurmond opposed his suggestion, saying it "would improperly interfere with the independence of the judicial branch of the government." The amendment failed, fifty-five to thirty-eight.[50]

As the 1993 Congress convened, another round of legislation was on the floor for consideration in the House and Senate. It ranged from amendments designed to alter the Constitution to resolutions that express the sense of the Congress but carry no legal force. Some proposed, once again, "voluntary prayer." Rep. Bill Emerson of Missouri said he was "introducing a constitutional amendment to allow communities to decide for themselves whether or not they will offer a benediction at their public ceremonies and graduations and whether their children will be able to voluntarily pray in school." His move was prompted by the *Lee v. Weisman* decision of 1992.

Sen. Thurmond brought up the same measure he had first introduced in 1983. He asserted once more that his amendment would restore a right taken away by a court that has "too broadly interpreted the establishment clause of the First Amendment."

Sen. Helms introduced two resolutions that propose an amendment to "restore the right of Americans to pray in public institutions, including public school graduation ceremonies and athletic events." Viewed in the late winter of 1993, there seems scant chance that any of these measures will find an attentive committee or large block of representatives or senators. And no longer do such proponents have a supportive voice in the White House.

Lee v. *Weisman*—End and Beginning

Almost thirty years to the day after the *Engel* decision of June 25, 1962, the Supreme Court, on June 24, 1992, handed down its opinion in *Weisman.*

The facts in the case are simple. "School principals in the public school system of the city of Providence, Rhode Island, are permitted to invite members of the clergy to offer invocation and benediction prayers as part of the formal graduation ceremonies for middle schools and for high schools."[51] In June 1989, at a graduation that included Deborah Weisman, Rabbi Leslie Gutterman was asked to deliver prayers, which he did. Since Deborah and her father objected, the school board sought to protect itself by supplying the rabbi with prayer guidelines composed by the National Conference of Christians and Jews. This was presumed to avoid offense. The Weismans, who are Jewish, knew that the principal had chosen a rabbi in order to cater to their complaints about an earlier graduation for Deborah's older sister, when a Baptist preacher had been explicitly Christian in his prayers. They told the principal that he just did not understand that they were dealing with a principle that went beyond personal wishes.

When the Weismans took the school to court they succeeded in getting a district court to enjoin the school "from continuing the practice at issue on the ground that it violated the Establishment Clause." The court of appeals affirmed that decision. The Bush administration urged the school officials to appeal and offered the highest level of assistance. In spite of that strong endorsement, the Supreme Court surprised most experts by voting five to four to support the Weismans. Justice Anthony Kennedy wrote for the majority,

> The sole question presented is whether a religious exercise may be conducted at a graduation ceremony in circumstances where, as we have found, young graduates who object are induced to conform. No holding by this Court suggests that a school can persuade or compel a student to participate in a religious exercise. That is being done here, and it is forbidden by the Establishment Clause of the First Amendment. For the reasons we have stated, the judgment of the Court of Appeals is Affirmed.[52]

It was a fitting conclusion to a bitter struggle, fitting if one happens to agree with the five-justice majority. But whichever side one adopts, it seems clear the curtain has been drawn on one chapter in the conflict between the Court and Congress.

In his argument before the Court on behalf of Lee in November 1991, U.S. Solicitor General Kenneth Starr, speaking for the Bush administration, was asked by one of the justices whether he urged the Court to reconsider *Engel*. "Starr said no, because the government opposes coercion."[53] He said, when asked by Justice O'Connor how *Engel* differed from a graduation ceremony, that in *Engel*'s classroom setting, a "powerful, subtle, indirect pressure" inheres in such factors as mandatory attendance and teacher

oversight. "Is classroom prayer compelled by the teacher unconstitutional?" asked Justice Stevens. "Yes," Starr replied, "because
it is coercive."[54]

The other attorney for the school board, Charles Cooper,
speaking to the press after oral arguments in November 1991,
asserted, "The classroom context is clearly a coercive context."

After all the bitter denunciations of *Engel*, the comparison
of the justices to communists, the claim that deity had been kicked
out of public schools, after all that and much more, the nation's
highest-ranking attorney, speaking for the Reagan/Bush agenda,
which included a school prayer amendment to correct *Engel* as
a top priority, set it all aside by agreeing fully with the decision
in *Engel*. Why Starr chose to do that we can only speculate.
The administration had committed itself to the overturning of
the three-part *Lemon* test.[55] It was a primary goal in going to
the Supreme Court on behalf of the school. Starr had challenged
the Court to overturn the *Lemon* test and replace it with a coercion
test, which, he believed, would allow the graduation prayer at
issue. Perhaps he felt the necessity to put *Engel* behind him
because he was so sure of winning the *Weisman* decision.

In finding against *Lee* the majority of the Court made it clear
that there would be no return to the *Engel* decision for restatement.
And the surprise in it all was that Justices Stevens and Blackmun
were joined not only by Justice O'Connor, but by Reagan appointee
Kennedy and Bush appointee David Souter. It was the same
coalition that would just a few days later reaffirm the constitutional right to an abortion in a Pennsylvania case. Religiously
motivated advocates of constitutional amendments supporting
prayer in schools and making abortion as nearly illegal as
possible, had lost their battles in the waning days of their twelve-
year access to presidential power. Of course they did not know
or perhaps even dream that within six months President Bush

would be bidding farewell to the White House. It is hard to imagine a more powerful engine of policy making being made available to school prayer advocates than they had from 1981 through 1992.

President Clinton has already committed himself against aid to parochial schools. His Baptist heritage, reaffirmed in Culpeper, Virginia, just prior to his inauguration, makes him a potential advocate of separation in the tradition of Roger Williams, John Clarke, John Leland, and Jimmy Carter. In sum, the dire predictions, in which I joined in 1980, suggesting that even eight years of a Reagan presidency would reshape the Supreme Court for decades, have been proven wrong. But only just barely, one might add.

The surprise for the long future is Justice Souter. He has already carved out a position on church/state issues that will provide a role of leadership in the post-Blackmun/Stevens era. Justice O'Connor is a reasonable, conservative justice. She will not likely trade away the separation heritage. Justice Kennedy, it appears, found his independent voice in 1992. Predictions are foolish, but there is reason to think that he may join his colleague in a continued moderate center of a Court that will undoubtedly see a more liberal cast of new appointees in the coming years. Finally, Justice Ruth Bader Ginsburg will almost certainly be of a different mind on church/state cases than was retired Justice White, whom she replaces.

Notes

1. The Senate approved S. 450 on April 9, 1979, by a vote of sixty-one to thirty after Sen. Helms attached his amendment on the floor.

2. U.S. Congress, House, Hearings before the Subcommittee on Courts, *Prayer in Public Schools and Buildings—Federal Court Juris-*

diction, 96th Congress, July 29, 1980, pp. 2-3.

3. Ibid., p. 7.

4. Ibid., p. 10.

5. Ibid., p. 12.

6. Ibid., p. 174.

7. It should be noted that the National Association of Evangelicals did continue its line of connecting the Court's decision with trends in Russia. Ibid., p. 216.

8. Ibid., p. 152. Bright had reversed his plagues. King was killed in April, Kennedy in June. But God is probably oblivious to calendar time.

9. Rep. Kastenmeier's question to Professor Rice. Ibid., p. 229.

10. Ibid., p. 335.

11. Depending upon the expert consulted, that help was major or minor. Either way, it energized a block of voters that would become a powerful force in the Republican Party in the succeeding twelve years.

12. In a 1980 pamphlet published by Moral Majority and entitled "Prayer: The Greatest Force for Change," Falwell wrote, "Only those who have been born-again by placing their faith in Jesus Christ can effectively call upon God to bless our nation." At the Lynchburg convention I recorded the remarks that included his exclusion of Jews.

13. Bob Slosser, *Reagan Inside Out* (Waco: Word Books, 1983). See also John Herbers, "Reagan Beginning to Get Top Billing in Christian Bookstores for Policies," *New York Times*, September 28, 1984, p. A23.

14. "Vice President Bush Appeals for 'Welcome' to Religious Right," *Religious Herald*, June 24, 1982, p. 12.

15. "White House Intervened with SBC Resolutions Committee," *Religious Herald*, July 15, 1982, p. 3. McAteer confirmed his role in this affair in his testimony before the Senate Judiciary Committee in July 1982. He stated, "Recently at the Nation's largest evangelical convention, the Southern Baptist's Convention, when the question was properly framed, when the agenda for the debate was properly set, overwhelmingly the people when they were asked what they thought about voluntary prayer, they voted 3 to 1 in favor of this constitutional

amendment" (U.S. Congress, Senate, Hearings before the Committee on the Judiciary, *Proposed Constitutional Amendment to Permit Voluntary Prayer*, 1982, p. 142).

16. "'Thousands Flock to Baptist 'Shoot-Out,' " *The Richmond News Leader*, June 11, 1985, p. 1.

17. Donald Rothberg, Associated Press dispatch, October 30, 1983.

18. U.S. Congress, Senate, Hearings before the Subcommittee on the Constitution, *Constitutional Restraint Upon the Judiciary*, 1981, p. 2.

19. Ibid., p. 99.

20. Ibid., p. 82.

21. "Senate Kills School Prayer for Session," *Washington Post*, September 24, 1982, p. 1.

22. *Congressional Record*, September 23, 1982, S.12022–23; 120937.

23. U.S. Congress, Senate Judiciary Committee, *Voluntary Prayer*, 1982, p. 1.

24. Ibid., pp. 1–2.

25. Ibid., p. 3.

26. Sen. Hatfield was sounding the call for action that would lead to the passage of the Equal Access Act on August 11, 1984. Many religious organizations representing a broad spectrum of ideologies endorsed the act at the time. It was designed to eliminate "perceived widespread discrimination" against religious speech in public schools. In 1990, by a vote of eight to one, the Supreme Court upheld the constitutionality of that act. In *Westside Community Schools* v. *Mergens* the Court approved a "limited open forum." This applies to a public secondary school when it offers opportunity for one or more "noncurriculum related student groups" to meet on school premises during noninstructional time. The forum is "limited" because it is available only to the school's own students. The school is not required to create a limited open forum, but if it does it may not discriminate against a student group because of the content of its speech. Finally, students themselves must seek permission to meet and they alone will direct and control the meetings. Teachers and other school employees may not initiate or direct the meetings, nor may outsiders.

On February 24, 1993, the Supreme Court heard arguments in the case of *Lamb's Chapel* v. *Center Moriches Union Free School District* that extends the issue to outside groups seeking use of school property. Lamb's Chapel was seeking access during nonschool hours when the building was the functional equivalent of a municipal auditorium. Those filing amicus briefs on behalf of Lamb's Chapel included the American Civil Liberties Union. and People for the American Way. The Court, in the summer of 1993, upheld Lamb's Chapel.

27. McClellan was so ill-informed about history that he asserted that after Madison had written his *Memorial and Remonstrance* Jefferson "further embellished" Madison's 1785 accomplishments by coming forward "with a proposal advocating complete religious freedom for all religious sects and for all dissenters. Entitled, 'An Act Establishing Religious Freedom.' " Of course, Jefferson had written that document in 1777 and it was Madison who achieved its passage in 1785.

28. U.S. Congress, Senate Judiciary Committee, *Voluntary Prayer,* 1982, p. 79.

29. Ibid., pp. 107–108.

30. Ibid., p. 160.

31. Ibid., p. 250.

32. For many Virginia residents there was little argument there.

33. U.S. Congress, Senate Judiciary Committee, *Voluntary Prayer,* 1982, p. 387.

34. "School Prayer Constitutional Amendment Report," January 24, 1984, p. 28.

35. U.S. Congress, Senate, Hearings before the Subcommittee on the Constitution, *Voluntary School Prayer Constitutional Amendment,* 1983, p. 64.

36. Ibid., p. 202.

37. Ibid., p. 212.

38. Ibid., p. 322.

39. Ibid., p. 366.

40. U.S. Congress, House, Hearings before the Subcommittee on Elementary, Secondary, and Vocational Education, *Religious Speech*

Protection Act, 1984, p. 96.

41. The legislation was passed in July and signed into law by the president on August 11, 1984.

42. U.S. Congress, Senate, Hearings before the Subcommittee on the Constitution, *Issues in Religious Liberty*, 1984, p. 195.

43. Senate Joint Resolution 165 authorized President Reagan to proclaim 1983 the "Year of the Bible." It was historically and conceptually a grievous error, compounded by the use of the flagrant religious language. It called the Bible the "Word of God" and called for the nation to renew its "knowledge and faith in God." For which faith did the Senate become a missionary? At best the "Year of the Bible" was meaningless political rhetoric, a mockery of religion and state alike. At worst, it reflected an agenda of change totally contradictory to constitutional guarantees. See Robert S. Alley, "The Founding Fathers and Religious Liberty," *Free Inquiry* 3, No. 2 (Spring 1983): 4–5.

44. Here Titus was likely referring to equal access. Two months after his remarks an Equal Access Act was passed with the support of many of the "others" Titus noted (U.S. Congress, Senate, *Issues in Religious Liberty*, p. 195). In 1993, Titus was dismissed as dean and professor from Pat Robertson's Regent University Law School. Titus wrote in October 1993, "Could it be that Pat Robertson is taking a lesson from Bill Clinton and moderating his principled views to find a place in the political middle, as identified in the most recent scientific poll?" (*The Forecast* [edited by Herbert Titus] 1, no. 1 [Oct. 1, 1993]: 2)

45. *Congressional Record*, 99th Congress, 1st Session, 1985, vol. 131, no. 1, S.20.

46. U.S. Congress, Senate, Hearings before the Judiciary Committee's Subcommittee on the Constitution, *Voluntary Silent Prayer Amendment*, June 19, 1985, p. 3.

47. Ibid., p. 14.

48. Ibid., p. 42.

49. Ibid., pp. 90–91.

50. Of the thirty-eight, twelve were Democrats, almost all of whom

came from Southern states. Conversely, twelve Republicans voted against the Helms amendment.

51. "*Lee v. Weisman,*" *United States Law Week,* June 23, 1992, vol. 60, no. 50, p. 4723.

52. Ibid., p. 4728.

53. "Arguments Before the Court—Benediction at Graduation Ceremony," *United States Law Week,* November 12, 1991, vol. 60, no. 19, p. 3352.

54. Ibid.

55. In *Lemon v. Kurtzman,* 1971, Chief Justice Warren Burger wrote for the majority focusing on "the three main evils against which the Establishment Clause was intended to afford protection: . . . Every analysis in this area must begin with consideration of the cumulative criteria developed by the Court over many years. Three such tests may be gleaned from our cases. First, the statute must have a secular legislative purpose; second, its principal or primary effect must be one that neither advances nor inhibits religion; finally, the statute must not foster 'an excessive government entanglement with religion.' " See Robert S. Alley, ed., *The Supreme Court on Church and State* (New York: Oxford University Press, 1988), p. 99.

12

The Sound of Silence

Closing Notes

As we have explored the past thirty years of debate over public school prayer two religious attitudes, both Protestant, have
been much in evidence. Both have roots in seventeenth-century
New England Puritanism.

First, the New Israel perspective, intolerant to a fault, repre-
sents a legitimate, if constitutionally rejected, part of the American
heritage. Second, filtered through colonial growth, the fires of
the Great Awakening, the Revolution, constitution building, and
Protestant pluralism, there emerged a voluntary principle in religion that tended to confine exclusive truth claims to personal
witnessing to fellow citizens in a secular state. The emerging
nineteenth-century Protestant hegemony was constrained, sometimes against its will, by the democratic traditions it helped foster.
True, its legacy fueled the messianism of Woodrow Wilson, but
a growing variety of religious traditions affected mainstream
Protestant leadership, which would learn to work within the con-

stitutional system.

Comfortable in a new position of influence in the body politic, many influential clergy, who were concurrently involved in the new ecumenicity, called for a "decent" separation between church and state. Indeed, it became a badge of honor to champion that separation. Successively mainstream Protestant leaders and scholars came to terms with biblical criticism, evolution, and, ultimately, a pluralistic, post World War II society.[1]

By 1962 the most prominent mainline churches of Protestant persuasion were heirs to several decades of ecumenical cooperation. Identified with the National and World Council of Churches, spokespersons for the large denominations saw themselves, it seems, as elders advising the Senate and the House membership to exercise restraint in efforts to tamper with the First Amendment. Many of them were aware of the strength their churches had drawn from the voluntary principle of association and were not eager to restore competition at the public till. They were also approaching the high-water mark of participation in the civil rights movement.

While the upscale Protestants were adjusting to such roles, the less visible and politically noninvolved fundamentalists, outcasts from what they perceived to be a wayward Protestant liberalism, wrote and preached against what they saw as the evils of the social gospel, biblical criticism, and the National Council of Churches. Literalist-driven theology spawned an angry challenge to the mainstream. In the 1950s the National Association of Evangelicals, firmly committed to strict Calvinist theology, accused its "liberal," neo-orthodox counterparts of undermining democratic values and being at least "soft" on communism. The loudest, most strident, and widely respected voice of that tradition was Billy Graham. But his success was in no small measure a result of a conscious effort to draw upon the mainline ministers to promote his crusades in city after city. Nevertheless, his message was a barrage of condemnations of biblical scholarship and a general contempt for preaching on social issues. In those years Graham saw no connection between his message and racial justice. His single target was communism and his sole weapon was decisions for Christ, which would turn the United States to his Christian God. We have commented on how that message became a part of the Eisenhower agenda. Few national commentators aside from Reinhold Niebuhr anticipated the mischief this simplistic fundamentalism would cause in the next decade.

These Protestant crosscurrents collided in 1962 with the *Engel* decision. Denominational and National Council leaders firmly supported the Court and so testified. Simultaneously, there was a strong grass roots resistance that found a voice in Billy Graham and Norman Vincent Peale. But uncompromising Protestant fundamentalism, within a few years, would find more dependable leadership among a cadre of television preachers who loathed accommodation with mainstream Protestants. Locking on to the *Roe* v. *Wade* decision of 1973, Jerry Falwell tapped a nascent anger in the disenfranchised fundamentalists. The result was the coalescing of the religious right and its new social agenda, ultimately honored by President Reagan, the first White House occupant to ignore the Protestant mainstream.

This fundamentalist force proclaimed an overt Christian exclusivism. It rested on an arrogant presumption of absolute truth riveted in the notion that divine revelation is singular, possessed only by those who have accepted fundamentalist dogma. It presumed that the ideal state was a Christian state. Virulent in expression, it found nurture in the same mentality that motivated much of the anti-Semitism that early became a foundation stone of traditional Catholic and Protestant theology.

Of course, the fundamentalists were merely reviving in new

directions a bitter conflict of the early church. Established orthodoxy successfully eliminated competing theological theories and trashed all deviations as heresy. A singular failure in that "holy" crusade was the effort to eliminate Judaism. The strength of the Jewish tradition has offered a persistent voice in contrast to Christianity for nearly two thousand years. Layers of prejudice and hate grew from those Christian leaders who saw the existence of Judaism as a badge of dishonor, a sign of failure. Thus was hatched a special breed of anti-Semitism spawned within Christian communions. The unspeakable horrors of the Holocaust have made nineteenth-century-style expressions of anti-Jewish prejudice impolitic in the modern church. However, it has persisted in genteel form in many walks of modern life. A prime example has been Christian disregard for the rights of Jewish citizens in the public schools. That residual venom was once again evident in private and public responses surrounding *Weisman*. It surfaces quickly whenever Jewish citizens claim rights under the religion clauses.

All too frequently such reactions are fueled by Christian religion teachers who assert "academic" distinctions between Jewish and Christian scholars. Such teachers, driven by a confessional imperative to "witness" to their students, may insist that no Jew can teach a university New Testament course as well as an equally trained Christian. This is, of course, a corruption of the academic profession. Oddly, many such individuals have no problem with a Christian teaching courses in Judaism. The perpetuation of a basic anti-Jewish sentiment appears to emerge from a simplistic claim that Jesus is God and the Jews reject him! Since the majority of American citizens are at least nominally Christian, such attitudes in the academy or the pulpit encourage discrimination in the pew. The poison of this exclusivistic religion may then infest the body politic, threatening to tear at the fabric of our secular, constitution-based democracy.

As the public has slogged its way through thirty years of debate over prayer in public school classrooms, self-appointed political protectors of public morality, most of them self-styled Christians, have successively advanced legislation to incorporate in those classrooms everything from prayer, to nonsectarian prayer, to nondenominational prayer, to voluntary prayer, to silent prayer, to silent meditation or prayer, to a moment of silence. While the battle was joined once again in 1993, the momentum has abated as former allies have shifted focus seeking to preserve a semblance of faith on the fringes. In 1993 the Rutherford Institute issued the following advisory on baccalaureate services. "These services are undoubtedly constitutional; . . . However, although such services are constitutional, there are limits on who may organize the services and where they may be held."[2]

No one should presume that by such publications fundamentalist leaders and their supporters have surrendered on the prayer-in-the-classroom issue, but the tide is running swiftly against those who would harbor hopes of reversing *Engel* and *Schempp*. Indeed, as we have noted, the Bush administration cast its lot with arguments in *Weisman* that admit the unconstitutionality, in principle, of school-sponsored classroom prayers. The U.S. Justice Department appears to have believed it would win the argument to abandon the *Lemon* test in 1992. Relying upon the conviction that Justice Kennedy would vote to apply a coercion test in the graduation arena and, further, that such a test would allow practices proscribed in *Weisman*, they were likely shocked by the Kennedy majority opinion.

The classroom prayer advocates were somewhat in disarray in the fall 1992. Two more blows came in rapid succession after the election of President Clinton. In March 1993, Justice Byron White announced his retirement. His vote, with rare exceptions, was with the Court accomodationists. Suddenly *Weisman* became a five-to-three decision. In a press conference a week later, President Clinton singled out the religion clauses of the First Amendment, noting that any nominee to the Court must be a strong advocate of religious freedom and the right to privacy. The appointment of Justice Ginsburg and Attorney General Janet Reno along with constitutional law experts closest to the president give reasons to conclude that the tradition of Justices Hugo Black, William Douglas, Earl Warren, William Brennan, Henry Blackmun, Thurgood Marshall, Lewis Powell, and John Paul Stevens is ascendant for the near future. And, somewhat surprisingly for many, Justice Souter has emerged as a thoughtful exponent of that separationist position:

> Forty-five years ago, this Court announced a basic principle of constitutional law from which it has not strayed: the Establishment clause forbids not only state practices that "aid one religion . . . or prefer one religion over another," but also those that "aid all religions." (*Everson v. Board of Education*) Today we reaffirm that principle, holding that the Establishment clause forbids state-sponsored prayers in public school settings no matter how nondenominational the prayers may be. In barring the State from sponsoring generically Theistic prayers where it could not sponsor sectarian ones, we hold true to a line of precedent from which there is no adequate historical case to depart.[3]

Souter also rejected unequivocally the notion of nonpreferentialism, a concept endorsed by Chief Justice William Rehnquist. Souter wrote, "Thus, on balance, history neither contradicts nor warrants reconsideration of the settled principle that the Establishment Clause forbids support for religion in general no less than support for one religion or some." His words in this case presage a position of leadership for Souter in church/state cases for the long future.

If, as now seems clear, the long debate over prescribed prayer in classrooms has subsided and the near future bodes well for supporters of the principle enshrined in *Engel,* what particular reasons have there been to retrace the thirty-year conflict? At least three come to mind.

First, only as the issue was joined in the years subsequent to *Engel* was it possible to incorporate in the public record substantial citizen response. That record will assist future generations in exploring the emotions and the arguments that engulfed the nation in a bitter struggle. It is no less important to have access to that record than to possess the debates in Congress over the passage of the religion clauses in 1789. Professor A. E. Dick Howard, distinguished constitutional authority at the University of Virginia, likes to talk about decisions that "take" and those that, on occasion, do not "take" with the public. That winding process of absorption is absolutely essential to a credible court. Whether *Engel* has taken or not, time will tell. But the process is well underway.

Second, the legislative debates provide a window on the social, political, intellectual, and religious attitudes of the post *Engel* era. They offer an extended portrait of mainstream Protestant leadership in the United States, not always in tune with constituents. The sudden emergence of the religious right is recorded in the long days of hearings in the eighties. The tomes of constitutional scholars are encapsulated in the testimony of dozens of legal experts.

Third, the record is a potential guide for future representatives and senators who, without doubt, will face similar issues of consequence, in succeeding decades. In sum, the testimony is both a glimpse of the mood of the nation and, perhaps, the education of a nation.

A commentator pleased with the most recent decision of the Court and the current trend in national politics can afford to be sanguine. Twelve years ago that was hardly the case. Faced with Supreme Court appointments from a president committed to a prayer amendment, uneasiness and fear for the First Amendment was predominant in the separationist camp. Many felt that were the Reagan-Bush control to extend for twelve years, the country would face decades of compromise with and accommodation to religion by the Court. In those years five justices were nominated, enough, with the elevation of William Rehnquist to chief justice, to redirect the Court on all manner of issues well into the twenty-first century. It was often noted after 1985 that the bitter dissent of Rehnquist and Scalia in the *Jaffree* case was only a harbinger of a solid majority of the Court that would come to agree, "The 'wall of separation between church and state,' is a metaphor based on bad history, a metaphor which has proved useless as a guide to judging. It should be frankly and explicitly abandoned."[4] Unlikely as it seemed then, three of the five new appointees in the Reagan/Bush years would supply the solid center for the majority in the 1992 *Weisman* decision.

The ruins of yesterday's reasonable fears is fair warning to those gripped by reasonable optimism in 1993. Conversely, the misery of those who plaintively ask, "What happened to Justice Kennedy?" will most assuredly not mark an end to their continued efforts to "put God back in the public schools." Indeed, the fight for prayer at graduation and baccalaureate services is currently in full bloom.

The challenge for advocates of voluntary religion in a free secular state is to make the case that only such a constitutional arrangement will secure freedom and effectively enhance the environment for vigorous religious activism and belief. It is not enough to take heart in a victory, for it already is in the past.

In 1960 Adlai Stevenson warned his fellow citizens that its "little aims and large fears" contained the seeds of destruction. This is time neither for complacency nor gloating.

Cultural Partitions and Democratic Traditions

The religious right has joined eagerly those decrying an emphasis upon cultural diversity. That critique has deterred many academic liberals from addressing the excesses of what has now been identified as multiculturalism. Contrasted with the arrogant white male mentality that presumed superiority of a single cultural heritage, the new movement espouses considerable wisdom. But it has a significant down side, one that may be traced to earlier days of the Republic.

In 1861 a group of southern states, supporting a kind of nineteenth-century strict cultural identity, sought to obstruct the natural application of the Bill of Rights. They desired that regional identity prevail over national constitutional principles. They envisioned a caste system of cultures—superior and inferior. Time and democratic values have proved Lincoln to be correct. A common commitment to democratic ideals provided a springboard for return to the Union by the recalcitrant states. To be sure, the South remained unremittingly racist in its public policy for another century. Even after the Supreme Court *Brown* v. *Board of Education* decision of 1954, leaders in the South promoted restrictive cultural blindness, insisting that blacks be separated from the white majority. While the Constitution ultimately prevailed, it was with some severe regional scars remaining. Martin Luther King, Jr. envisioned a nation of diversity guaranteed by the good will of common commitment to constitutional principles belonging to us all. "I have a dream that one day, on the red hills of Georgia, sons of former slaves and the sons of former slave owners will be able to sit down together at the table of brotherhood." King spoke of the "oasis of freedom and justice." In the final analysis, without that nurturing common source, there is nothing to assure the vitality of our great experiment in democracy.

In a recent volume, *Culture of Complaint*, Robert Hughes makes a similar point.

> It is too simple to say that America is, or ever was, a melting pot. But it is also too simple to say none of its contents actually melted. No single metaphor can do justice to the complexity of cultural crossing and perfusion in America. American mutuality has no choice but to live in recognition of differences. But it is destroyed when those differences get raised into cultural ramparts. . . . We now have our own conservatives promising a "cultural war," while ignorant radicals orate about "separatism."[5]

The 1954 Supreme Court accepted a modified melting principle as applying to all citizens. For decades bitter resistance to that decision doomed the cautious vision of the nine justices. The 1968 murder of King dimmed the hopes for *Brown* v. *Board of Education* "taking" with the nation. King's assassination seemed to give the country over to a counter melting pot, the mentality of J. Edgar Hoover, who posited different degrees of citizenship. That same mindset prevailed among many who sought to have the nation conform to some general religion by enforcing prayer in schools. Sen. Helms, like Hoover, championed a vision of enforcement to bring about uniformity.

King understood the melting pot theory in a profound way. His rhetoric employed the biblical legends and stories, but he transformed them into metaphors in his quest to explicate and extol the constitutional principle for which he gave his life. Justice, freedom, equality—those were the virtues of the secular republic for which he stood.[6]

With all the debate about multiculturalism lately, little time is devoted to the genius of this nation's own culture, its secular democracy. The Bill of Rights is the envy of cultures around the world. Most often the Supreme Court has recognized the wonder of that heritage. Respect for genuine cultural pride in this pluralistic nation is long overdue. But as authors such as Richard Rodriguez have insisted, such pride must not allow the American democratic heritage to be discarded in the name of diversity.

Today clever politicians and scholarly nitpickers have sought to impose consensus religion and/or politically correct speech in the nation. Both derive from the same arrogant, exclusivistic, fundamentalist root, dividing a nation, and destroying freedom.

A recent example of this mood to be found in scholarly circles is the work of Professor David M. Smolin of Samford Law School. In an extended review of Michael Perry's *Love and Power: The Role of Religion and Morality in American Politics,* Smolin advocates a return to a federalism where the local majority ordains the extent of freedom available to the minority. His astounding conclusion: "Certainly, minorities within states retain their civil and political rights, as suggested above. Nonetheless, in the battle over defining and effectuating the temporal peace, one option of losers should be the traditional American remedy of migration."[7] With this remarkable appellation—"losers" for minorities within a state—perhaps Smolin could use a variation of the old sixties bumper stickers, "Alabama, Love it or Leave it."

In March 1993 a group of youth ministers in the Richmond, Virginia, area organized to retain official school-sponsored baccalaureate services. Their reasoning was remarkable. "If we continue these radical efforts to avoid pressuring children to be religious, we actually teach and enforce notions that pressure the young to avoid all that is religious." Why, the letter asked, "should a minority rule the majority, and the majority be punished?"[8]

From earliest times the United States has possessed dozens of discreet cultures. Now they number in the hundreds. Of all nations on the globe this one of ours may be the most diverse in ethnic and cultural traditions. It is troubling that after two centuries of struggle the United States embarks upon its third hundred years by being called back to absolutist claims created out of cultural diversity that would mock our common experience. For our current inquiry that absolutism is manifest in religious claims that we have heard in the thirty-year debate over school prayer.

The framework of constitutional government as defined in the United States depends for its stability upon the central thesis that a republican (representative) democracy is the most appropriate and effective means of self-government. Remove that assumption and replace it with dependence on "leadership" only at the presidential level and the constitutional system becomes a fragile institution indeed.

In most respects cultural diversity has heavily affected the 535 elected representatives from the fifty states. Most of the elected officials are torn by special interests that admit to no common threads. Single-issue politics, whether focused upon ethnic, racial, religious, or ideological differences, threatens to fracture the very core of the system. It is the excessive demand by every tiny segment of the electorate, each dominated by a single issue, not only to be represented but also to be supported by votes cast, that has driven politicians to micropolitics, a politics that must balance the innumerable special interests. The diverse, exclusive demands of special interests destroy capacity for leadership in the process of exercising their will.

As a result the entire notion of politics as a profession is swallowed in references to public opinion polls. Television, consistently focused on the sound bite policy that enhances the celebrity status of the newsperson, tries to extract the most quotable line from the hapless politician. The art of governance is not allowed to prosper largely because television news gatherers have little if any understanding of the nature of constitutional government in a republican democracy. More and more voters identify themselves as "independent," by which they often mean "ignorant."

Returning to King, he comprehended his religion, his heritage, and his constitution. He envisioned an American culture that celebrated diversity and he knew where the enemies lay. In his 1963 *Letter From Birmingham Jail* King prophetically warned:

I am further convinced that if our white brothers dismiss as "rabble-rousers" and "outside agitators" those of us who employ nonviolent action, and if they refuse to support our non-violent efforts, millions of Negroes will, out of frustration and despair, seek solace and security in black-nationalist ideologies—a development that would inevitably lead to a frightening racial nightmare.

The dream was spoken again by Barbara Jordan when she keynoted the 1992 Democratic Convention by hailing both diversity and unity. She proudly proclaimed "E pluribus unum." Unreasoning political correctness divides. Whether motivated by religious arrogance, cultural pride, racism, or academic ideology, it denies King's dream, a dream grounded in the Madisonian principles of democratic republicanism.

In matters of religion in our pluralistic democracy, extreme ethnic and cultural pride can cause destructive results comparable to the religious conflicts, too numerous to name, that dot the globe in 1993. Insistence upon a single religion, a Christian nation, seeks to enforce a totalitarian melting pot. Seeking to mollify opponents, the broadening of the religious net through nonsectarian language is a false accommodation. Fundamentalist leaders call for abolition of the public schools and the balkanizing of education along religious and cultural lines.

Since 1962 many members of Congress and millions of citizens were, in the words of Simon and Garfunkel, "hearing without listening" to the Supreme Court. The Court was writing "songs voices never shared." The popular sixties song, "The Sound of Silence," still haunts a generation. Whatever the messages intended by the two young men, silence was perceived as having enormous power. In our current public conflict it seems the First Amendment has, perhaps, at long last conveyed to the Congress the admonition to be silent. It would be a resounding silence in the name of freedom and equality. It is that same silence that the Court has reserved for every child without regard to belief or persuasion. For public schools, its obvious corollary is voluntary silent meditation, something always available in our republican democracy. It might be argued that the American cultural legacy is simply a reasoned governmental silence in the arena of constitutional free speech and conscience. That in turn will spawn the untamed rough and tumble debate over ideas that is the genius of our democratic heritage. Multiple cultures and regions are secure only so long as the Constitution remains a common inheritance for all citizens. The roots of democratic freedom lie neither in dogma nor doctrine, of whatever stripe, but reside rather in our common constitutional heritage of a secular republic. That is a theme we cannot do without!

Notes

1. In March 1993 two distinguished Christian leaders, Episcopal Bishop John Spong and New Testament scholar John Maquarrie, appeared in academic settings in Richmond, Virginia. Both made explicit their rejection of the assertion that Jesus claimed deity for himself. Such forthright challenges to "orthodoxy" remain all too rare among Christian preachers and teachers.

2. *Baccalaureate Services, The Constitutionality of an American Tradition* (Charlottesville, Va.: The Rutherford Institute, 1993). The conclusions reached were heavily based upon the decision in *Lee v. Weisman*. In an undated flyer on the same subject Pat Robertson's legal arm, the American Center for Law and Justice, played on the theme of "the firmly established free speech rights of students."

3. Justice Souter's concurring opinion joined by Justices Stevens and O'Connor.

4. Chief Justice William Rehnquist's dissent in *Wallace v. Jaffree* (1985).

5. Robert Hughes, *Culture of Complaint* (Oxford University Press, 1993), pp. 12–13.

6. Unfortunately, since the early 1950s young citizens have been denied the cadence that made that portion of the pledge of Allegiance so compelling. By injecting "under God" the primal thought is lost. Such surgery suggests that only theists can affirm "one nation, indivisible, with liberty and justice for all."

7. David M. Smolin, "Regulating Religious and Cultural Conflict in a Postmodern America: A Response to Professor Perry," *Iowa Law Review* (1991): 1102–1103. It is hard to believe that it took Smolin thirty-seven pages to arrive at this conclusion.

8. Form letter distributed by the Richmond Area Youth Ministers Association at Branch's Baptist Church, March 18, 1993. It was to be sent to school officials by as many persons as possible.

Appendix A

A *Memorial and Remonstrance* by James Madison

Commentary by Robert Alley*

The *Memorial and Remonstrance* both affirmed the principle of religious freedom and helped to defeat the Assessment Bill. It memorialized the General Assembly, offering fifteen remonstrances against the proposed Assessment Bill.

In his introduction to the list of remonstrances, Madison explained that the signers of the petition took action because they believed the Assessment Bill would constitute a "dangerous abuse of power." The remonstrances that follow this declaration comprised a list of reasons for this judgment. In the first remonstrance, Madison made three points: that religion can only be directed by conviction and reason; that "Civil Society" has no

---

*this Constitution, fall 1986, No. 12, pp. 28–33 (published by "Project '87" of the American Historical Association and the American Political Science Association).

role to play with respect to religion; and that permitting the majority to rule absolutely can result in the destruction of rights of the minority. In the second remonstrance he contended that if the legislature passed the bill, it would be exceeding its lawful authority.

We the subscribers, citizens of the said Commonwealth, having taken into serious consideration, a Bill printed by order of the last Session of General Assembly, entitled "A Bill establishing a provision for Teachers of the Christian Religion," and conceiving that the same if finally armed with the sanctions of a law, will be a dangerous abuse of power, are bound as faithful members of a free State to remonstrate against it, and to declare the reasons by which we are determined. We remonstrate against the said Bill,

1. Because we hold it for a fundamental and undeniable truth, "that Religion or the duty which we owe to our Creator and the manner of discharging it, can be directed only by reason and conviction, not by force or violence." [Article XVI, Virginia Declaration of Rights] The religion then of every man must be left to the conviction and conscience of every man; and it is the right of every man to exercise it as these may dictate. This right is in its nature an unalienable right. It is unalienable, because the opinions of men, depending only on the evidence contemplated by their own minds cannot follow the dictates of other men: It is unalienable also, because what is here a right towards men, is a duty towards the Creator. It is the duty of every man to render to the Creator such homage and such only as he believes to be acceptable to him. This duty is precedent, both in order of time and in degree of obligation to the claims of Civil Society. Before any man can be considered as a member of Civil Society, he must be considered as a subject of the Governour of the Universe: And if a member of Civil

Society, who enters into an subordinate Association, must always do it with a reservation of his duty to the General Authority; much more must every man who becomes a member of any particular Civil Society, do it with a saving of his allegiance to the Universal Sovereign. We maintain therefore that in matters of Religion, no man's right is abridged by the institution of Civil Society, and that Religion is wholly exempt from its cognizance. True it is, that no other rule exists by which any question which may divide a Society can be ultimately determined, but the will of the majority; but it is also true that the majority may trespass on the rights of the minority.

2. Because if Religion be exempt from the authority of the Society at large, still less can it be subject to that of the Legislative Body. The latter are but the creatures and vicegerents of the former. Their jurisdiction is both derivative and limited: it is limited with regard to the co-ordinate departments, more necessarily is it limited with regard to the constituents. The preservation of a free Government requires not merely, that the metes and bounds which separate each department of power be invariably maintained; but more especially that neither of them be suffered to overleap the great Barrier which defends the rights of the people. The Rulers who are guilty of such an encroachment, exceed the commission from which they derive their authority, and are Tyrants. The People who submit to it are governed by laws made neither by themselves nor by an authority derived from them, and are slaves.

In the third argument, which contains in the first sentence Madison's most often quoted phrase, he warned against allowing any government interference with human rights, a lesson learned, he said, in the recent Revolution. An authority that taxes for the support of Christianity, may "with the same ease" later choose to establish a single Christian sect. (This is the most telling argument against nonpreferentialism.)

3. Because it is proper to take alarm at the first experiment on our liberties. We hold this prudent jealousy to be the first duty of Citizens, and one of the noblest characteristics of the late Revolution. The free men of America did not wait til usurped power had strengthened itself by exercise, and entangled the question in precedents. They saw all the consequences in the principle, and they avoided the consequences by denying the principle. We revere this lesson too much soon to forget it. Who does not see that the same authority which can establish Christianity, in exclusion of all other Religions, may establish with the same ease any particular sect of Christians, in exclusion of all other Sects? that the same authority which can force a citizen to contribute three pence only of his property for the support of any one establishment, may force him to conform to any other establishment in all cases whatsoever?

At this point Madison argued that individuals possess equal natural rights to their religious beliefs and he refined earlier arguments made by persons such as Roger Williams, as he insisted that coercion in religion is an offense against God.

4. Because the Bill violates that equality which ought to be the basis of every law; and which is more indispensible, in proportion as the validity or expediency of any law is more liable to be impeached. If "All men are by nature equally free and independent," all men are to be considered as entering into Society on equal conditions; as relinquishing no more, and therefore retaining no less, one than another, of their natural rights. Above all are they to be considered as retaining an "equal title to the free exercise of Religion according to the dictates of Conscience." [Virginia Declaration of Rights.] Whilst we assert for ourselves a freedom to embrace, to profess and to observe the Religion, which we believe to be of divine origin, we cannot

deny an equal freedom to those whose minds have not yet yielded to the evidence which has convinced us. If this freedom be abused, it is an offence against God, not against man: To God, therefore, not to man, must an account of it be rendered. As the Bill violates equality by subjecting some to peculiar burdens, so it violates the same principle, by granting to others peculiar exemptions. Are the Quakers and Menonists the only sects who think a compulsive support of their religions unnecessary and unwarrantable? Can their piety alone be intrusted with the care of public worship? Ought their religions to be endowed, above all others, with extraordinary privileges by which proselytes may be enticed from all others? We think too favorably of the justice and good sense of these denominations to believe, that they either covet pre-eminences over their fellow citizens, or that they will be seduced by them, from the common opposition to the measure.

Madison addressed the twofold issue of establishment and free exercise in remonstrance five. He provided here a strong argument for the protection of the state from religion, and he labeled as a "perversion" of religion its use to achieve political ends.

5. Because the Bill implies either that the Civil Magistrate is a competent Judge of Religious Truth; or that he may employ Religion as an engine of Civil policy. The first is an arrogant pretension falsified by the contradictory opinions of Rulers in all ages, and throughout the world: the second an unhallowed perversion of the means of salvation.

Madison was seeking signatures from Baptists and Presbyterians. The sixth paragraph appealed to their concerns by making the Christian argument for religious freedom. Madison contended

that Christianity does not require state support in order to flourish
and that seeking it demeans its divine nature. Once again Roger
Williams comes to mind. Madison continued this line of argument
in remonstrance twelve.

> 6. Because the establishment proposed by the Bill is not
> requisite for the support of the Christian Religion. To say that
> it is, is a contradiction to the Christian Religion itself, for every
> page of it disavows a dependence on the powers of this world:
> it is a contradiction to fact; for it is known that this Religion
> both existed and flourished, not only without the support of
> human laws, but in spite of every opposition from them, and
> not only during the period of miraculous aid, but long after
> it had been left to its own evidence and the ordinary care of
> Providence. Nay, it is a contradiction in terms; for a Religion
> not invested by human policy, must have pre-existed and been
> supported, before it was established by human policy. It is
> moreover to weaken in those who profess this Religion a pious
> confidence in its innate excellence and the patronage of its
> Author; and to foster in those who still reject it, a suspicion
> that its friends are too conscious of its fallacies to trust it to
> its own merits.

In remonstrance seven Madison argued that state support
historically has damaged the Christian cause.

> 7. Because experience witnesseth that ecclesiastical estab-
> lishments, instead of maintaining the purity and efficacy of
> Religion, have had a contrary operation. During almost fifteen
> centuries has the legal establishment of Christianity been on
> trial. What have been its fruits? More or less in all places, pride
> and indolence in the Clergy, ignorance and servility in the laity,
> in both, superstition, bigotry and persecution. Enquire of the

Teachers of Christianity for the ages in which it appeared in
its greatest lustre; those of every sect, point to the ages prior
to its incorporation with Civil policy. Propose a restoration of
this primitive State in which its Teachers depended on the
voluntary rewards of their flocks, many of them predict a
downfall. On which Side ought their testimony to have greatest
weight, when for or when against their interest?

Contrary to some modern interpreters, Madison was not only
concerned over interference by the state into church affairs, he
was equally disturbed over the prospect of religious institutions
working their will on the civil government. If religion does not
require state assistance, he asserted, good government does not
need assistance from an established religion.

8. Because the establishment in question is not necessary
for the support of Civil Government. If it be urged as necessary
for the support of Civil Government only as it is a means of
supporting Religion, and it be not necessary for the latter
purpose, it cannot be necessary for the former. If Religion be
not within the cognizance of Civil Government how can its
legal establishment be necessary to Civil Government? What
influence in fact have ecclesiastical establishments had on Civil
Society? In some instances they have been seen to erect a
spiritual tyranny on the ruins of the Civil authority; in many
instances they have been seen upholding the thrones of political
tyranny; in no instance have they been seen the guardians of
the liberties of the people. Rulers who wished to subvert the
public liberty, may have found an established Clergy convenient
auxiliaries. A just Government instituted to secure & perpetuate
it needs them not. Such a Government will be best supported
by protecting every Citizen in the enjoyment of his Religion
with the same equal hand which protects his person and his

property; by neither invading the equal rights of any Sect, nor suffering any Sect to invade those of another.

Madison next pointed out that the "generous policy" of freedom from religious establishment in the nation offered asylum to persecuted persons abroad, promising a "lustre" to our country. To tax for support of religion would drive potential immigrants to other states, and encourage native Virginians to leave.

9. Because the proposed establishment is a departure from that generous policy, which, offering an Asylum to the persecuted and oppressed of every Nation and Religion, promised a lustre to our country, and an accession to the number of its citizens. What a melancholy mark is the Bill of sudden degeneracy? Instead of holding forth an Asylum to the persecuted, it is itself a signal of persecution. It degrades from the equal rank of Citizens all those whose opinions in Religion do not bend to those of the Legislative authority. Distant as it may be in its present form from the Inquisition, it differs from it only in degree. The one is the first step, the other the last in the career of intolerance. The magnanimous sufferer under this cruel scourge in foreign Regions, must view the Bill as a Beacon on our Coast, warning him to seek some other haven, where liberty and philanthropy in their due extent, may offer a more certain repose from his Troubles.

10. Because it will have a like tendency to banish our Citizens. The allurements presented by other situations are every day thinning their number. To superadd a fresh motive to emigration by revoking the liberty which they now enjoy, would be the same species of folly which has dishonoured and depopulated flourishing kingdoms.

George Washington referred to the destruction of harmony among religious sects when he observed that he wished the Assessment Bill had never been introduced. Madison follows that idea by noting that only religious freedom and equality among religions assures domestic peace.

> 11. Because it will destroy that moderation and harmony which the forbearance of our laws to intermeddle with Religion has produced among its several sects. Torrents of blood have been spilt in the old world, by vain attempts of the secular arm, to extinguish Religious discord, by proscribing all differences in Religious opinion. Time has at length revealed the true remedy. Every relaxation of narrow and rigorous policy, wherever it has been tried, has been found to assuage the disease. The American Theatre has exhibited proofs that equal and complete liberty, if it does not wholly eradicate it, sufficiently destroys its malignant influence on the health and prosperity of the State. If with the salutary effects of this system under our own eyes, we begin to contract the bounds of Religious freedom, we know no name that will too severely reproach our folly. At least let warning be taken at the first fruits of the threatened innovation. The very appearance of the Bill has transformed "that Christian forbearance, love and charity," [Virginia Declaration of Rights] which of late mutually prevailed, into animosities and jealousies, which may not soon be appeased. What mischiefs may not be dreaded, should this enemy to the public quiet be armed with the force of law?

Appealing at this point to the missionary zeal of the dissenters, Madison insisted that making Virginia a Christian state would discourage non-Christians from migrating. This, in turn, would hinder the ability to spread the gospel. Madison's language in this section was cast in evangelical terms and there is no evidence that the narrow gauge religious exclusivism he painted had any relation to his own thoughts. He was making the Baptist case.

12. Because the policy of the Bill is adverse to the diffusion of the light of Christianity. The first wish of those who enjoy the precious gift ought to be that it may be imparted to the whole race of mankind. Compare the number of those who have as yet received it with the number still remaining under the domination of false Religions; and how small is the former! Does the policy of the Bill tend to lessen the disproportion? No; it at once discourages those who are strangers to the light of revelation from coming into the Religion of it; and countenances by example the nations who continue in darkness, in shutting out those who might convey it to them. Instead of levelling as far as possible, every obstacle to the victorious progress of Truth, the Bill with an ignoble and unchristian timidity would circumscribe it with a wall of defence against the encroachments of error.

The Assessment Bill was unwise, Madison wrote, because so many Virginians will find it "obnoxious" that it will be unenforceable.

13. Because attempts to enforce by legal sanctions, acts obnoxious to so great a proportion of Citizens, tend to enervate the laws in general, and to slacken the bands of Society. If it will be difficult to execute any law which is not generally deemed necessary or salutary, what must be the case, where it is deemed invalid and dangerous? And what may be the effect of so striking an example of impotency in the Government, or its general authority?

Madison was even willing to argue that the majority did not favor this bill, a risky digression given his contention that the majority should not be allowed to decide matters of natural rights. What logical action would follow if the majority clearly favored assessment? It was a gamble. He was dealing with an assembly that took public opinion quite seriously and he undoubtedly was banking on overwhelming popular opposition to assessment. He was correct.

14. Because a measure of such singular magnitude and delicacy ought not to be imposed, without the clearest evidence that it is called for by a majority of citizens, and no satisfactory method is yet proposed by which the voice of the majority in this case may be determined, or its influence secured. "The people of the respective counties are indeed requested to signify their opinion respecting the adoption of the Bill to the next Session of Assembly." [From a resolution by opponents of assessment passed by the General Assembly in October 1784, that staved off enactment of the Assessment Bill that year.] But the representation must be made equal, before the voice either of the Representatives or of the Counties will be that of the people. Our hope is that neither of the former will, after due consideration, espouse the dangerous principle of the Bill. Should the event disappoint us, it will still leave us in full confidence, that a fair appeal to the letter will reverse the sentence against our liberties.

Returning to his basic themes, Madison concluded with a ringing defense of natural rights, warning the Virginia Assembly that it had no authority to "sweep away all our fundamental rights." If it could establish a religion, it could then, if it wished, eliminate trial by jury. Madison reminds us that religious freedom is, in its origin, "the gift of nature," and once more he affirmed that, in his view of deity, such freedom of conscience is the only policy consistent with that deity. He argued not from dogma, but from reason and natural rights. By so doing he established a portrait of a creator consistent with such rights.

15. Because finally, "the equal right of every citizen to the free exercise of conscience" is held by the same tenure with all our other rights. If we recur to its origin, it is equally the gift of nature; if we weigh its importance, it cannot be less dear to us; if we consult the "Declaration of those rights which pertain to the good people of Virginia, as the basis and foundation of Government," it is enumerated with equal solemnity, or rather studied emphasis. Either then, we must say that the Will of the Legislature is the only measure of their authority; and that in the plenitude of this authority, they may sweep away all our fundamental rights; or, that they are bound to leave this particular right untouched and sacred: Either we must say that they may control the freedom of the press, may abolish the Trial by Jury, may swallow up the Executive and Judiciary Powers of the State; nay that they may despoil us of our very right of suffrage, and erect themselves into an independent and hereditary Assembly or, we must say, that they have no authority to enact into law the Bill under consideration. We the Subscribers say, that the General Assembly of the Commonwealth have no such authority. And that no effort may be omitted on our part against so dangerous an usurpation, we oppose to it, this remonstrance; earnestly praying, as we are in duty bound, that the Supreme Lawgiver of the Universe, by illuminating those to whom it is addressed, may on the one hand, turn their Councils from every act which would affront his holy prerogative, or violate the trust committed to them: and on the other, guide them into every measure which may be worthy of his (blessing, may re) dound to their own praise, and may establish more firmly the liberties, the prosperity and the happiness of the Commonwealth.

Appendix B

Testimony of Robert S. Alley
before the Senate Subcommittee
on Constitutional Amendments,
August 8, 1966

With reference to the proposed amendment to the First Amendment of the United States Constitution, I respectfully offer to
the committee the following reasons for its rejection.

I.

The amendment as phrased and as regularly described by its
proponents, including Senator Dirksen of Illinois, is quite obviously religiously motivated. No matter how bland this religious
quality may prove to be, it justifies the contention that the Dirksen
amendment is in itself a violation of the First Amendment to
the Constitution. It undertakes to establish that which is clearly
prohibited. Therefore, the proposed action would alter radically

the character of the First Amendment. Of course, I do not suggest that the Congress and the people are precluded from such an alteration if accomplished through constituted means. However, it is in order to hear the words of Thomas Jefferson in remarks referring to the Virginia Bill for Establishing Religious Freedom. Mr. Jefferson observed, "The rights hereby asserted are of the natural rights of mankind and that if any act shall be hereafter passed to repeal the present or to narrow its operations, such act will be an infringement of natural rights." Let us make no mistake, the passage of the amendment under consideration would, no matter how slightly at first, prevent the free exercise of religion and, no matter how innocuous, establish a form of religion.

II.

This means that the First Amendment, which has stood as a protection of all minorities, would be limited to the protection of those only who have some religious sentiment. Only the human rights of "religious" persons would have absolute protection. Such a situation would be a complete reversal of the intention of the founding fathers who specifically rejected the idea of multiple or plural establishment.

III.

The proposed amendment would drastically affect future Supreme Court decisions based upon the First Amendment. In the past the justices have found satisfactory basis for interpretation in the historic background out of which the First Amendment originated. This has proved sound footing for the preservation of the principle of religious liberty as expressed in the separation of church and state. One need only cite a few of the many decisions in the present century in which reference to James Madison and Jefferson have been determinative. Even the slightest alteration in the First Amendment would eliminate this sure foundation. The Supreme Court would be faced with a changed document which must in some degree indicate dissatisfaction with the original. Thus the basic human rights guaranteed in the Bill of Rights would be qualified. Intended or not, this is a predictable result.

The earliest members of this great body insisted upon careful safeguards for the minority of the citizenry. Such wisdom saw that the soundest basis for the liberties of the many was the assurance of freedom for the minority. Indeed the majority requires protection from its worst corporate self and therefore essential human rights are not subject to the whim of the majority.

IV.

The proposed amendment speaks of prayer. What is prayer? Is it religious exercise? If not, then what? What kind or kinds of prayer are involved here? These questions must be considered as unanswered by the proponents of the amendment. As a free citizen of the United States I have chosen to be a Christian. This is my religious faith. Prayer for the Christian necessarily involves the person of Jesus Christ. Every religious faith defines the essence of prayer differently. For me there is no such thing as general or non-sectarian prayer. It either is in keeping with my own convictions or it is not prayer for me. Therefore, the promotion of prayer—and we can hardly see this amendment in other light— by the federal government inevitably raises questions not alone for the atheist, but for the religious person as well. I have two sons. The oldest boy begins first grade in September. My wife and I seek to create what we believe to be a Christian environment for our children. I would resist as a basic violation of my conscience and that of my son his subjection to "non-sectarian" prayer. It would be, for him, another religion more akin to a national cult than to the faith of the New Testament. In short, if the prayer is not clearly and unapologetically sectarian it will violate my conscience and if it is of such character then it will necessarily violate the conscience of my neighbor who is not a Christian.

V.

It may be argued that this proposal only seeks the permission of "voluntary" prayer. But the word voluntary has never been adequately defined. Senator Dirksen insists that the common man will have his way on this matter. But what does the average citizen mean by voluntary? I suggest that often the average citizen means by voluntary that the teacher may pray if he or she wishes. I have talked to many persons who have so expressed themselves. But of course this is hardly voluntary for the students. It may be insisted that voluntary means the class deciding to pray. Does this mean majority rule while the rest close their ears or step outside? Or is this to be construed as meaning unanimous consent of students and teacher? If the latter, it requires no insight to recognize how quickly this method may become coercive where only one or two children differ from the vast majority.

When I was in the third grade in a Richmond area elementary public school a religion course with non-denominational Protestant bias was taught in the building during school hours. If parental permission was not given to enroll the child he could sit on the steps for forty minutes exercising his freedom. My father, always strongly committed to religious liberty, did not desire me to be in the class and thus did two boys sit on the steps and talk each day. As the days passed my friend and I were subjected to various remarks. I have forgotten what was said to me, but I remember to this day the afternoon I asked my father, "What is a Jew?" My friend was the son of devout Jewish parents whose conscience would not allow them to enroll him in the class. As a result he was singled out and identified as peculiar. Now, this boy was indeed free not to take the class. But at what price? I have seen coercion among children and well know how difficult it is to be set apart as different. The Dirksen amendment is an open invitation to such coercion, if not outright persecution. The only meaningful definition of the word voluntary as related to prayer in the public schools is in terms of the individual. Voluntary prayer may be the free individual, teacher or pupil, uttering a private petition. But is not the First Amendment as it is the most adequate document ever produced by man to protect that right of voluntary prayer? The Supreme Court has never so much as hinted that true voluntary prayer could be prohibited. Obviously it could not be. I believe the proposal to be corrosive of human rights, but even at best it is totally superfluous.

VI.

If, as I believe, this proposed amendment is intended to inculcate moral values then it is a clear violation of the spirit of the First Amendment. Historian Perry Miller, in writing concerning Roger Williams, remarked that Williams' greatest contribution was his insistence over against the Massachusetts Bay religious leaders, that genuine morality, goodness, and religious commitment gave these men no right "to impose upon others their own definitions." The God whom I worship is not a subject of legislation.

It is interesting to note that recent studies of Roman Catholic parochial schools in this country by the University of Chicago indicate a disappointing lack of success in the stimulation of religious response. Are we to assume that a watered-down, brief devotional period in the public schools will produce any positive results? As a matter of fact, the large majority of students whom I have taught at the University of Richmond who had been subjected in the public schools to morning devotions have become sickened by such group prayer and are admittedly bored presently with all devotions. My experience has shown all such efforts at infused piosity to produce negative results.

I am in agreement with Professor Winthrop Hudson in his suggestion that the distinctive concept in America is the "voluntary" principle in religion. The Supreme Court has consistently interpreted the Constitution in light of Jefferson's wall of separation. Our very society is presently indebted to this concept. It was precisely because many of the early statesmen were religious men that they saw the necessity of the First Amendment. It would be ironic if we were to lose our cherished tradition by adopting the so called "voluntary" prayer amendment. At the same time that the Senate and the House are wisely extending the legislation to guarantee civil rights, let it not, in the same decade, find cause to restrict basic human rights.

Appendix C

Testimony of Professor Norman Redlich, American Jewish Congress Senate Hearings, Committee on the Judiciary, September 16, 1982

I believe that this proposed amendment strikes at the very heart of the basic concepts of religious freedom in this country. I have been fortunate to grow up in a country where there are no preferred religions, where we are all equal before the law, where there are no prescribed religious faiths, or prescribed ceremonies that have the imprimatur of government.

It is no accident that this country alone, among countries, has the kind of commitment that we do, to separation of church and State, and is at the same time the country where religious freedom flourishes as it does nowhere else on Earth.

I do not want to be a religious stranger in this country, and I do not want my children or grandchildren to be religious strangers in this country.

Permit school boards, whether in Brooklyn or in Utah, to adopt prayers of the majority, and have Mormon prayers in Utah, and Jewish prayers in New York, then whether they be Catholics or Protestants or Jews, in some parts of this country they will be religious strangers in their own home. There is no way that cannot be coercive.

If the establishment clause was based on any values at all in our history, it was based on the value of neutrality, it was based on the value of no prescribed religious faith, and it was based on the value of no coercion. In those three essential respects, this proposed constitutional amendment violates some of the basic precepts of religious freedom in this country, and religious freedom, I may add, is not something that is only a religious concept, it is a political concept.

Every totalitarian government must do away with religious freedom, because religious freedom recognizes an authority that the government cannot control; that is why every totalitarian State either controls religion, subverts religion, or creates a State religion. It cannot put up with a religion that is free, and not controlled by the State.

When the founders put the religious clauses first in the first amendment, it was because of a clear recognition that freedom of religion was essential to political democracy, and the establishment clause and the free exercise clause were a recognition of the essential nature of religious freedom as part of our political framework, and a recognition that the government had to remain neutral, government could not coerce, and government could not prescribe a faith.

This proposed amendment permits those things to happen.

Now, one could quarrel with individual decisions of the Supreme Court on any particular matter. I happen to think that the Supreme Court was correct in its *Engel* v. *Vitale* and *Schempp* decisions, because they were faithful to the principles of the establishment clause. But I would say, even if one disagrees with particular interpretations, the worst criticism—the worst that one could say the court is guilty of, is like Othello, that perhaps they loved religious freedom, not wisely, but too well. I happen to think they loved religious freedom both wisely and well, and an excessive concern for religious freedom, and religious neutrality, is not something that the Congress should correct by constitutional amendment; it is something that we should all accept, we should all tolerate, and all be very proud of, and Mr. Chairman, I urge the rejection of this proposal.

Appendix D

The Free Exercise Crisis

In the Senate hearings of 1984 an attorney from Harrisburg, Pennsylvania, William Ball, a constitutional expert, was joined by Laurence Tribe of Harvard in a lengthy discussion with the Senate committee. They were talking about governmental interference in religious activities. Ball was speaking of a Nebraska case in which he was soon to be involved. He noted, "The State's obligation was to prove that it had a compelling State interest in imposing these laws on religious ministries, and the schools had the obligation of proving that they were indeed religious ministries, and I think the church carried its burden. The State did not carry its burden." Ball was assuming the established principle that when there are apparent violations of First Amendment rights the state must give the highest scrutiny to its actions and show a compelling interest that overrides a fundamental constitutional right.

On April 17, 1990, the Supreme Court made its ruling on the *Employment Division of Oregon* v. *Smith* case. Five of the six justices in the majority asserted that state law may override a free exercise of religion claim without resorting to the highest scrutiny and without demonstrating a compelling state interest. Justice O'Connor vigorously dissented from their premise but found a compelling interest in the *Smith* case. In writing for the majority Justice Antonin Scalia suggested that accommodation of religious minorities should be left to the state political process. If the law in question was not designed to deny rights under the First Amendment then a mere accidental impact did not require the state to show evidence of compelling interest.

In fact, this ruling reduced First Amendment guarantees to the level of incidental state legislation, where the state law was to take precedence. O'Connor argued that the majority had erred by overturning established precedents. She wrote, "The First Amendment was enacted precisely to protect the rights of those whose religious practices are not shared by the majority and may be viewed with hostility." Justices Harry Blackmun, William Brennan, and Thurgood Marshall in dissent argued that the majority overturned "a settled and inviolate principle of this Court's First Amendment jurisprudence," and showed little "judicial restraint."

Response to the decision was instant and massive from all segments of the religious community, right to left, as well as from leading constitutional law experts. All agreed the decision expanded state power at the expense of individual liberty. Quickly a coalition was formed to ask the Court to reconsider its decision. The coalition consisted of a massive number of organizations, left and right. In June the Court denied the request.

On July 26, 1990, Rep. Stephen Solarz of New York introduced the Religious Freedom Restoration Act in the House, cosponsored by thirty-four members. RFRA stated that the government may not restrict a person's free exercise of religion unless the restriction is in the form of a generally applicable law that furthers a compelling state interest and is the least restrictive means to achieve that goal. The act allowed those who believed their religious rights were violated to bring a civil action in the courts. At that time Solarz predicted quick passage.

In May 1991 Justice O'Connor spoke to a gathering in Philadelphia and addressed the *Smith* decision. "The free exercise clause does not mean very much if all a state has to do is make a law generally applicable in order to severely burden a very central aspect of our citizens' lives." Further, the implications for future establishment cases are distressing.

On June 26, 1991, Rep. Solarz reintroduced RFRA in the House. It was noted that *Smith* had already had an impact on some twenty lower court decisions. A snag was encountered when some pro-life supporters suggested the act might be used to create a constitutional right to abortion were *Roe* v. *Wade* to be overturned. In spite of enormous activity by advocates of the act it failed of passage again in 1991–92. On May 13 and 14 the House Subcommittee on Civil and Constitutional Rights held hearings on the act. Nadine Strossen, president of the American Civil Liberties Union, testified, "We invest government with broad and important powers that sometimes override individual liberty. It should, however, not be easy for government to do so—or official bodies will use that power with substantial frequency." In a similar vein the position of the Bush administration, espoused in its arguments in the *Lee* v. *Weisman* case, sought a looser standard on establishment cases, but the Court, in 1992, failed to follow the Justice Department's lead.

The election of 1992 brought to the White House a president committed to passage of RFRA. He had so indicated in a September 1992 speech before Jewish leaders. It is now anticipated that Congress will pass RFRA in 1993 and that it will be quickly signed by President Clinton.

Select Bibliography

The author of this book has developed a thesis that results in a particular point of view for which he makes a case. The volumes listed here are but a sample of dozens of works on the subject of school prayer and reflect other perspectives and assumptions resulting, in some instances, in quite different conclusions. It is assumed that the interested reader can determine this without intrusive annotations by the author.

Alley, Robert S. *The Supreme Court on Church and State.* New York: Oxford University Press, 1988.

Boston, Robert. *Why the Religious Right Is Wrong about Separation of Church and State.* Buffalo, N.Y.: Prometheus Books, 1993.

Buckley, Thomas E. *Church and State in Revolutionary Virginia.* Charlottesville: University Press of Virginia, 1977.

Cord, Robert L. *Separation of Church and State: Historical Fact and Current Fiction.* New York: Lambeth Press, 1982.

Curry, Thomas J. *The First Freedoms: Church and State in America to the Passage of the First Amendment.* New York: Oxford University Press, 1986.

Dolbeare, Kenneth M., and Phillip E. Hammond. *The School Prayer*

Decisions. Chicago: University of Chicago Press, 1971.

Handy, Robert T. *A Christian America: Protestant Hopes and Historical Reality*. New York: Oxford University Press, 1984.

Ivers, Gregg. *Redefining the First Freedom: The Supreme Court and the Consolidation of State Power*. New Brunswick, N.J.: Transaction Publishers, 1993.

Ketcham, Ralph. *James Madison*. Charlottesville: University Press of Virginia, 1990.

Keynes, Edward, and Randall Miller. *The Court vs. Congress: Prayer, Busing and Abortion*. Durham, N.C.: Duke University Press, 1989.

Laubach, John Herbert. *School Prayers: Congress, the Court, and the Public*. Washington, D.C.: Public Affairs Press, 1969.

Levy, Leonard W. *The Establishment Clause: Religion and the First Amendment*. New York: Macmillan, 1986.

———. *Original Intent and the Framers' Constitution*. New York: Macmillan, 1988.

Littell, Franklin H. *From State Church to Pluralism: A Protestant Interpretation of Religion in American History*. New York: Macmillan, 1971.

Malbin, Michael J. *Religion and Politics: The Intentions of the Authors of the First Amendment*. Washington, D.C.: American Enterprise Institute, 1978.

McLoughlin, William G. *New England Dissent, 1630-1833: The Baptists and Separation of Church and State*. Cambridge, Mass.: Harvard University Press, 1971.

Miller, Robert T., and Ronald B. Flowers. *Toward Benevolent Neutrality: Church, State, and the Supreme Court*. Waco, Tex.: Baylor University Press, 1993, Fourth Edition.

Miller, William Lee. *The First Liberty: Religion and the American Republic*. New York: Alfred Knopf, 1985.

Morgan, Richard E. *The Supreme Court and Religion*. New York: The Free Press, 1972.

Mulder, John M., and John F. Wilson, eds. *Religion in American History: Interpretive Essays*. Engelwood Cliffs, N.J.: Prentice-Hall, 1978.

Pfeffer, Leo. *Church, State and Freedom.* Boston: Beacon Press, 1967.

Rice, Charles E. *The Supreme Court and Public Prayer: The Need for Restraint.* New York: Fordham University Press, 1964.

Smith, Rodney K. *Public Prayer and the Constitution: A Case Study in Constitutional Interpretation.* Wilmington, Del.: Scholarly Resources, 1987.

Stokes, Anson Phelps. *Church and State in the United States.* New York: Harper & Brothers, 1950.

Whitehead, John W. *The Rights of Religious Persons in Public Education.* Wheaton, Ill.: Crossway Books, 1991.

Wood, James E., ed. *Religion and the State: Essays in Honor of Leo Pfeffer.* Waco, Tex.: Baylor University Press, 1984.

Index

263